Strategies to Overcome Stress

Guide for Anyone Who Wants to Manage and Fight Anger, Anxiety, Negativity. Methods to Feel Relief and Get a Stress Free Brain, Stop Procrastination and Addiction

David Michael King

© Copyright 2019 – All rights reserved

The content contained within this book may not be reproduced, duplicated or transmitted without direct written permission from the author or the publisher. Under no circumstances will any blame or legal responsibility be held against the publisher, or author, for any damages, reparation, or monetary loss due to the information contained within this book. Either directly or indirectly.

Legal Notice

This book is copyright protected. This book is only for personal use. You cannot amend, distribute, sell, use, quote or paraphrase any part, or the content within this book, without the consent of the author or publisher.

Disclaimer Notice

Please note the information contained within this document is for educational and entertainment purposes only. All effort has been executed to present accurate, up to date, and reliable, complete information. No warranties of any kind are declared or implied. Readers acknowledge that the author is not engaging in the rendering of legal, financial, medical or professional advice. The content within this book has been derived from various sources. Please consult a licensed professional before attempting any techniques outlined in this book. By reading this document, the reader agrees that under no circumstances is the author responsible for any losses, direct or indirect, which are incurred as a result of the use of information contained within this document, including, but not limited to, errors, omissions, or inaccuracies.

Table of Contents

Chapter 1: Introduction: The Common Triggers and Symptoms of Stress

Everyone at some point in their lives has felt stressed. It is an incredibly commonly used phrase that outlines an uncomfortable, unpleasant experience that manifests itself physiologically, emotionally, and psychologically. Unless you have been diagnosed with a specific personality disorder, such as psychopathy, which is defined by a severe void of stress, you can easily travel back in your mind to times when stress has overwhelmed you. What did it feel like? How long did it last? Did you know what was going on? How did your experience of stress vary from the one you were a child to grow into adulthood? And most of all, do you feel like stress is interfering with your day-to-day life and causing you to feel unproductive and discontent?

This book is going to help you identify your stressors and how you have learned to cope with them. It will then offer you fresh new methods of coping mechanism; ones that are much healthier and simple to apply. Once you continuously apply these techniques, you will find that they are morphing into habits that you happily participate in. These habits will teach you how to notice your own personal stress triggers, how to combat them once they arrive, and how to effectively manage both the physiological and psychological experiences of stress at the moment. We will also guide you in the direction of self-care and relaxation, helping you blend several practices into your daily life.

But first, we have to talk about what stress actually is, before you learn how to deal with it.

1.1 What is Stress?

Many people do not have a proper grasp on what the experience of stress actually looks like. Some people link together the experience of a panic attack, an extreme reaction to intense anxiety, as the visual representation of what stress manifesting itself outwardly may appear as.

Some people connect it to a mere physiological experience of neck pain, backaches, and consistent headaches that arrive once work begins. Others know when they are stressed because they begin craving a form of drugs or alcohol that will drown out their uncomfortable sensations.

Stress, in a tangible sense, is the experience of the neurochemical cortisol, firing out of the neurons in our brain and shooting down our brain stem. These elevated cortisol levels interfere with our memory, learning processes, lower immune function, and increase our blood pressure. This way if we are doing a speech in front of a group of people and we feel stressed, we may forget how to begin, because cortisol is rushing through our veins.

This is also why we sweat, our hearts race, and our thoughts tend to expand and run into each other. This combined physiological and psychological reaction to a stimulus is what evolutionists refer to as the fight-or-flight response; a fearful reaction that has been ingrained without human nature since the dawn of consciousness. What is does is warn us about potential threats and danger. Once we have assessed the threat, we can decide whether or not we want to fight it, or flee from it.

But what happens when stress manifests itself more severely, and also, through an extended period of time?

1.2 Different Kinds of Stress

Acute Stress: This kind of stress is the kind that is felt temporarily, and is experienced during fight-or-flight situations. It is immediate and very intense; it only lasts for a certain amount of time and fades when the stimuli go away, or when you begin to adjust to the stimuli. An example of this could be going for a job interview, or rushing to get to work on time. The majority of the time, these momentary experiences of stress does not adversely affect a healthy person. But there are more extreme moments that could affect a person for a lifetime, such as when a traumatic accident occurs to a person or a loved one. These people then become vulnerable to developing post-traumatic stress disorder, a mental health issue that is defined by this sudden onset of stress.

Chronic Stress: There is a reason why stress still exists as a bodily and emotional reaction in humans; it acts to benefit us in several ways still. It can motivate us, encourage us, and energize us into action when it is needed most, especially in an emergency. But stress turns into health issues when the stressors pile up, lingering inside a person's mind and thus their body. Persistent stress can lead to bodily symptoms that seem subtle, such as headaches and back pain, that come and go every now and then without a known definitive cause. The inability to deal with these stressors can also lead to other mental health problems, such as the experience of mood disorders like depression, and other anxiety disorders.

Take a mental note about the last time you felt stressed. How did you know you were stressed? What physical symptoms do you experience? Do you feel like you are suffering from acute stress or chronic stress? If you are unsure, you may want to purchase a blank notebook so you can begin making notes from now on while reading along in this book. Take note on the next sections on triggers and symptoms, writing down the ones you feel you experience most often. Once you write them down, put in brackets how often this actually is; it could daily, weekly, or occasionally (which would be once every two to three weeks).

1.3 Common Causes/Triggers

The first step in learning to manage your stress levels is to identify what triggers your stress experience. Everyone is going to have different triggers; some people may become very stressed about traffic jams, when their child doesn't clean up their toys, while others are not bothered in this slightest. Your life situation, environment, nature, and way you are nurtured are all going to factor in, which makes stress management, not a one-size-fits-all treatment plan. Be sure, to be honest with yourself within these next sections, as it will only benefit you in the future.

1.4 External Stressors

Major Life Changes: Changes in your life do not have to be negative in order to make you feel stressed. They can be a new engagement, planning a wedding, or a new job promotion. But of course, the negative changes would still affect you aversely, such as the death of a loved one, a breakup, or moving into another city/town.

1. The Environment: What is occurring on a consistent basis in the world around you can be a great source of stress. Some people are more sensitive and react

to the sudden sound of a barking dog, or the presence of too much light or dark within that room as well. Sometimes these things can be too stimulating, too loud, too overwhelming, to the point where some people experience the physical sensations of stress and don't realize what they are being stressed by.

2. Unpredictable Events: We cannot control everything that happens in our day to day lives. An unpredictable event can be something as small as a traffic accident or forgetting to buy wine for the guests who are coming over. It, of course, includes larger events, such as a pay-cut, a job firing, or the sudden presence of guests. What actually stresses a person and is unpredictable will depend upon the person and what they consider upsetting. One person may be okay with friends dropping by without an invite, whereas, this may stress out another person.

3. Workplace: The workplace is a very common source of external stress. Meeting deadline, keeping up a good work ethic, worrying about what your boss thinks of you, getting enough hours, dealing with customers, etc., are some examples of how the workplace can cause stress for any person.

4. Social: Meeting new people can very stressful for someone who has social anxiety, or even a person who simply doesn't engage with strangers very often. Going on a blind date would make most people stressed. Having to mentor someone at work and have them look up to you probably stresses many people as well.

1.5 Internal Stressors

Not all stress falls under the category of events that happen to us. Sometimes, we are the source of our stress, which often leads to the experience of mental health problems. The following list of internal stimuli is generalized for this section but will be expanded on in the later chapters of this book.

1. Fears: Having a specific fear or phobia can be a constant source of stress, especially if a person chooses to avoid it, and how often they are faced with it. A person can fear flying, snakes, public speaking, or a more generalized sensation of a fear of failure.

2. Uncertainty and lack of control: Most do not like when they are not at least even in moderate control

of what happens to them. This is when our imagination runs wild, and we construct the worst possible scenario. Not knowing whether or not you got a job, or are waiting for the results of a medical test, can cause a fair amount of stress.

3. Beliefs: This falls under the umbrella of attitudes, opinions, and expectations as well. Our beliefs shape our experiences and how we appraise them in our minds. Having the expectations that everything will go well may set us up for stressful feelings, as well as having an attitude that we only deserve good things, can cause stress to thrive inside us. (Cognitive distortions, as well as mistaken beliefs, will be discussed later on in this book.)

As previously mentioned, everyone can get stressed for different reasons. This list is a mere generalization of thousands of other external or internal stimuli that can cause a person stress. If you didn't see any of the main sources of stimuli that cause you to stress listed above, feel free to write your own list that is more specific.

1.6 Common Symptoms

The following list is symptoms of chronic and acute stress that may be going unnoticed in your life, beyond the obvious physical sensations of racing heart, shortness of breath, rapid thoughts, shaking hands and general anxiety.

1. Acne: This is one of the most visual ways that stress is able to manifest itself. This is believed to happen because when some people are stressed out, they tend to touch their face more often than usual, which leads to the spreading of bacteria that was on their hands. A correlation was made in a study that observed 22 people before and during an exam and noted an increase in acne severity. Another reason as to why this may occur is picking habits that some people in engage in when they are ruminating about something. The stress, of course, isn't the only cause of acne; many teenagers have acne due to hormonal shifts and excess oil production.

2. Headaches: Headaches can be caused by many external and internal stimuli, such as temperature changes, hydration issues, medication side effects, a head injury, etc. A study of 267 people with chronic

headaches found that a stressful event preceded the development of the chronic headache, in 45% of the cases. A larger study done in the United States surveyed over 150 million service members at a headache clinic and found that 67% of those who attended the clinic claimed that their headache was triggered by stress. This would make it the second most common headache trigger, the first being dehydration.

3. Chronic Pain: Random aches and pains without a known cause are a common issue amongst those with chronic stress issues. Studies have found that increased stress and physical pain may be associated with the presence of the stress hormone cortisol.

4. Frequent Sickness: If you are constantly calling in sick to work and feel you are always recovering from a cold or flu, you may be suffering from chronic stress issues. Stress has been known to deplete the strength of our immune systems and make us more susceptible to infections and viruses around us.

5. Decreased Energy and Insomnia: This is a symptom of many mental health disorders in general. The brain becomes overly tired from working overtime, and also loses healthy sleep time because the

person is ruminating over a stressful situation. People usually suffer from this particular symptom if they are going through a particularly stressful point in their lives, which can lead to depression, anxiety disorders, as well as other associated physical issues.

6. Changes in Libido: Many people have noted over years of research how their sex drive has diminished due to stressful life situations. This is why many couples do not engage in sexual activity as often when they have a baby because they are more consistently stressed than usual. This also happens because the hormone cortisol is present, and interferes with the hormones that are necessary for sexual arousal. This is most often the case for many women who are excessively stressed.

7. Digestive Issues: Problems such as having diarrhea and constipation have been linked to experiences of high stress. One study looked at 3,000 children who were exposed to stressful events and found that constipation was greatly associated with them. Stress may also more adversely affect those with digestive disorders such as irritable bowel syndrome (IBS), or inflammatory bowel disease (IBD). Both of

these disorders are characterized by stomach pain, bloating, diarrhea, and constipation.

8. Appetite Changes: This symptom is also another sign of depression. Many people who are stressed out before a big meeting, presentation, or job interview, will not eat breakfast in the morning because they find that they have no appetite. On the other hand, some people reach for food more often when they are stressed, depending upon what the stressful stimuli are. Increase in weight is very common during times of intense stress.

9. Depression: Depression has been mentioned several times throughout this section because it is directly linked to the experience of stress. Many studies have been done that have linked stressful life-events to the onset of depression, as well as the many symptoms of chronic stress being associated with the symptoms of depression. In general, if you are suffering from the symptoms of depression, you have probably experienced some form of chronic stress in your life.

10. Rapid Heartbeat: An increased heart rate can be a symptom of higher stress levels, not only in an acute manner but in a chronic way as well. Our heartbeats are naturally faster (unless you have a

specific personality disorder) when we are within stressful situations, or when we recall a stressful one.

11. Excessive Sweating: Sweating when engaging in physical activity or when you are nervous is entirely normal. Excessive sweating may mean that you are spending a lot of time thinking about the stressful event/situation, or you are engaging in one on a consistent basis. Excessive sweating can also be experienced by people with anxiety disorders, and also acts as a side effect for many medications.

12. Forgetfulness and Disorganization: If you are usually very organized, and are suddenly feeling very forgetful and disorganized, you may be experiencing chronic stress. Memory issues due occur from higher levels of cortisol, as well as when you do not get enough sleep.

13. Pessimistic Views: This is also a symptom of depression, and occurs often when a person has been experiencing a very stressful event and isn't coping with them. If you feel like you can only see the negative side of every coin, it may be time to start investigating what is causing you so much stress in your life.

14. Clenched Jaw and Grinding Teeth: Have you ever felt sore in your jaw and you don't know why? Have you ever woken up with a headache along with a sore jaw? You could be grinding your teeth in your sleep, or are doing it subconsciously while you ruminate about an issue that is stressing you out. This is very common for people with anxiety disorders and is a very difficult habit to start noticing and to break.

As previously mentioned, you could be experiencing other symptoms of stress that are not listed here. If you believe this is the case, write it down in your notebook, and how the same process as the other symptoms and triggers. Once you have done this, it is time to make a hierarchy.

Try to make a list of the top 10 triggers of stress in your life. Once you have found at least 10, rate them between 1-10, number 1 being the most stressful, and number 10 being the least. When you have this, be sure to keep it in the front of your notebook, as you will be referencing it often when asked to practice various techniques throughout this book.

And now, we will go forward onto your new journey of stress management!

One that is full of new and healthy habits, relaxation, and awareness!

Chapter 2: How to Develop a Rational Mind: Proven Techniques

The first way that you can begin to tackle your issues with stress is by becoming aware of the patterns that dominate your thinking style. You have grown up with a certain thinking pattern that has developed through being raised by your parents/caretakers, your own personal experiences, as well as your genetics. And this thinking pattern has a great deal to do with how you cope with stress. If you have decided to pick up this book, that probably means that your old way hasn't been working for you. In this section, you will learn how to begin becoming aware of the faulty thinking patterns that lead you to become more stressed, as well as ways to replace those faulty thinking patterns with more effective ones.

First, we will identify negative thinking patterns. These negative thinking patterns are best understood under the description of Cognitive Behavioral Therapy (CBT). CBT is a form of therapy that fuses together the concepts of thoughts, behavior, and emotions, are how they interchangeably affect one another. One of the main practices within this form of treatment asks the client to identify their faulty thinking patterns that may be encouraging the presence of their mood or anxiety disorder. These are called cognitive distortions, and many people fall under their toxic pattern without being aware of it. Some of the most common ones are listed as follows:

2.1 Cognitive Distortions

Cognitive distortions are described as inaccurate thoughts that reinforce negative thought patterns or emotions. They are faulty ways of thinking that convince the person of a reality that simply is not true. These are patterns of thinking that have been practiced for the majority of our lives, and thus makes it more ingrained into our perception of reality.

CBT seeks to address and restructure the process of thinking that involves these cognitive disruptions. First, the most common cognitive distortions will be listed and described. Later, exercises will be introduced that can help you identify your most applied cognitive distortions, and how you can challenge them.

1. Filtering: This refers to the tendency to only see the negative aspect of things throughout our day, our life, or a particular situation. For example, you may have been stuck in traffic, but you still managed to arrive on time for your event and had a good time. Some people who apply to filter may dwell on the fact that they were/are stuck in traffic and how much it distrusts their mood.

2. Polarized thinking ("Black and White" Thinking): This is the tendency to look at situations in two extreme ways; everything is either very bad or very good. There is nothing of a mixture in the middle. Either you had a great time at the party, or it was horrible.

3. Overgeneralization: This is when a person can take an incident and use it as the sole pieces of evidence that arrives upon a much broader conclusion. For example, a person may have been dating around, had one bad date, and concluded that they would never find a partner in life-based merely upon the experience of this one date.

4. Jumping to Conclusions: This is the act of feeling sure of something without evidence at all. This distortion can thrive within anxiety and depression, as the tendency to believe in imagined outcomes is

natural to the disorder. An anxious person may believe that they may get hit by a car crossing the street, or a depressed person may believe that they have no future at all.

5. Personalization: The belief that everything an individual does has a direct impact on external events or other people. The link is usually irrational. For example, a person with anxiety might believe that because they forgot to bring food to a party that everyone will not enjoy the party, because of their mistake.

6. Control Fallacies: This is the belief that everything that happens to us is either entirely our fault or entirely caused by forces outside of our control. What occurs in life is generally a combination of both? An example of this is believing that our work performance is because of our managers, or that mistakes made by others are caused by mistakes we made.

7. The fallacy of Fairness: This is an extreme take what is deemed 'fair' in life. The person believes that because they are a good person, or have done good things in life, they deserve to live a life that is fair. This is simply not the case as life goes on.

8. Blaming: When things do not go well, or we are not feeling right, a person who practices this cognitive distortion will look outward and blame others for how they act and what they are feeling.

9. Should: This distortion refers to the unspoken or spoken rules of how we believe in our culture or society should behave. When others break the rules, we are hurt. When we break our rules, we feel shame and guilt. This leads to unrealistic expectations of ourselves or others that are all mental rather than existing in reality. For example, we may feel guilty if we spend too much money on ourselves if we think overspending isn't okay. We may become angry at a waiter or waitress if we believe they 'should' be constantly filling up our water glass, but isn't.

10. Emotional Reasoning: This is the belief that if we feel a certain way, then it must be a true fact. For example, if we feel like something we said made us sound stupid, then we must indeed be stupid in reality. This is an incredibly common distortion that immediately connects emotions to facts. This is an important distortion to note before approaching the cognitive restructuring section of this chapter.

11. The fallacy of Change: This is the expectation that others should change in order to suit our needs. This connects to the feeling that our happiness depends highly on other people. This is a very unhealthy way to live because we cannot control others, and making them responsible for our happiness is simply not anyone else's duty but our own.

12. Global Labeling/Mislabeling: This is an extreme form of generalizing; this is where we take small instances of evidence and apply it on a global scale. You may have tried to learn to drive a few times in your life but conclude that you will never be able to drive due to these few experiences. It is exaggerated judgments based on the single occurrence, such as a person saying something slightly rude, and concluding that they are an overall bad person.

13. Always being Right: This distortion makes us believe that we must always be right in order to be happy. Some people have believed that being happy is more important than being kind to others, and have a difficult time admitting when they have made a mistake.

14. Heaven's Reward Fallacy: This involves the false belief that any act of self-sacrifice we commit will

pay off. Some may call this karma and will believe that there exists an immediate award, whether tangibly or in praise. This leaves a person bitter when they do not receive the reward that they are expecting.

15. Catastrophizing/Magnifying or Minimizing: This involves the expectation that the worst will always happen, or has already happened. This evidence will be based on the smallest incident that is much smaller than the person interprets it as. If you make a mistake at work, there exists a fear that you will get fired because of it. Minimizing is when a person does not focus on a positive occurrence in their life and downplays it to uncontrollable external forces rather than their own dedication or hard work.

2.2 Cognitive Restructuring: A Practice

Cognitive restructuring is a useful technique that helps you understand the underlying meanings behind your mood, thoughts, and behaviors. It is a life-long practice that challenges some of your most common cognitive distortions, sometimes called 'automatic thoughts/beliefs,' It can help you change the negative thinking that lies behind the experience of a down, angry, or anxious mood.

There are seven steps that you can apply while within the moment of experiencing a negative mood, such as anxiety, depression, and anger, or stress. These steps will be described and are meant to help your situational, along with deep breathing and relaxation exercises. We will later explore other thought-record/challenging exercise.

Here, I will use the specific example of a person with generalized anxiety, who feels triggered by having to eat in a public place. They are beginning to feel a panic attack coming on, and thoughts are racing through their head.

MindTools suggests the application of the six steps:

1. Calm Yourself: Deep breathing and meditation practices will be described in a later chapter that will help you feel better in the moment when a negative mood is triggered.
2. Identify the situation: Describe the situation that triggered your negative mood. In this case, it was

the abrupt realization that the person needs to eat lunch with a coworker or friend unexpectedly.

3. Analyze your Mood: Identify how you are feeling, and be honest about it. Moods are distinguishable from thoughts because they usually involve a single word. In this example, one word would be easy to identify; anxiety.

4. Identify Automatic Thoughts: Try to notice the automatic thoughts that are rising in your mind as your mood begins to come about. Some examples in this situation might revolve around the fear of judgment, the fear of having someone notice your anxiety, the fear of a panic attack, etc.

5. Find Objective Support Evidence: Find evidence that supports your automatic thoughts. Look at it objectively, without emotion. In this situation, a person may use examples of why the person may judge them, or that their eyes moved down to their shaky hands, etc. It would be important not to dwell on what we are assuming the other person is thinking of you because there exist no objective facts that say just that.

6. Find Objective Contradictory Evidence: When you arrive upon a balanced view, which is defined as seeing a situation as objectively as possible, which is

what it means to gather facts about a situation. This is meant to instill the notion that thoughts nor are emotions facts. In this example, the balanced thought may sound something like; "they may notice my anxiety, but that's okay," or "there is no evidence that tells me that they have noticed my anxiety, nor has it shown that they will disapprove of it." These replaced thoughts are meant to calm you down and bring you to a more even state.

It is recommended that after one of these episodes that you monitor your mood. You can do this through direct observation during an interaction, or after. Be sure to write this down as soon as you are able to have a moment to yourself. More of these achieved balanced thoughts written down will allow you to recognize how often you are able to help yourself, which in turn makes you feel less and less helpless in your experience of your mental health issue.

2.3 Noticing your Cognitive Distortions

It is going to take time and practice for you to get into the pattern of noticing when you are applying some of these cognitive distortions to yourself and your reality. Like any muscle, it needs to be exercised, trained, and flex. Before long, what initially took hours of note-writing will turn into a new, automatic way of thinking that happens inside of your mind within seconds.

The neural pathways in your brain have been so used to going in one direction, that the sudden desire to turn them the opposing way will surely cause some discomfort, emotionally and mentally. Give yourself some time, and don't be so hard on yourself. It took this amount of time for the cognitive distortions to build themselves into your experience of depression, anxiety, and anger, so it will take time for it to grow into more adaptive reactions. Habits take time to form, and there is no limit on the space of time necessary in order to execute change.

Try to bring your notebook with you wherever you go, or make a document on your phone where you can try noticing some of these cognitive distortions. Pay attention to what you say to yourself and what kind of emotions accompany these thoughts. Try to take note of how much these thoughts stress you on a particular day, on a scale of 1-10, 10 being the most stressful, 1 being the least amount of stress you could feel.

If you are having difficulty noticing your thoughts and how they correlate with your levels of stress, read on into the next section that will help you practice doing this.

2.4 How to Begin Noticing Your Stressful Thoughts: Mindfulness

The notion of mindfulness meditation will be discussed more in the later chapter on relaxation. But right now, we will focus on simply mindfulness; the practice of noticing.

Noticing what exactly? The answer to this in mindfulness is everything. If you don't know anything about mindfulness, you may think that you are already doing this. You are noticing the look your boss gave you in a meeting when you weren't completely paying attention, you noticed the new outfit your partner bought, you noticed the rain. While some of this may be true, you were probably more so, within the very definition of the word, seeing, rather than noticing.

Before you are able to begin practicing meditation, you need to learn how to challenge your thoughts. And before you can learn to challenge your thoughts, you have to notice the ones that are adversely affecting you, and thus making you more stressed. There is where mindfulness will help you.

Before we begin talking about meditation practices, there are ways in which you can begin being mindful about yourself in your everyday life. There are so many points in our lives where are merely existing, hovering on autopilot throughout the day, and barely being present to experience it. This happens often when people are driving to work, or taking transit, or even while feigning listening to another person while our minds wander off onto what needs to be done next. Most people in the Western world have a difficult time focusing, due to societal notions that being a 'work-a-holic' and constantly multitasking is a state to be honed after. But if you think about it right now as you are reading this book, those actions are more than likely the reasons why you are feeling how you are, right?

Mindfulness is usually described as the quality or state of being conscious or aware of something, and a mental state achieved by focusing one's attention in the present moment; all done while acknowledging the presence of thoughts, feelings, and bodily sensations. When we are multitasking, we are not focusing on one thing, and when we are ruminating, we are allowing ourselves to be taken away by our own thoughts. The entire point of mindfulness is not to rid yourself of thoughts that may make you feel negative; thinking patterns are harnessed by the warming of certain neural pathways and are not always within our control. But what we can control is how we choose to respond to them.

For example, you may have a thought arise in your mind on the weekend about the quality of a certain project in your work life. Perhaps you think something like, "maybe it won't be good enough, and the boss will think I didn't try hard enough." Wherever you are, no matter what you are doing externally, this thought is going to make you feel a negative emotion, such as guilt, anxiety, shame, etc.

If you are not mindful of this thought and how it is affecting your mood, it will take your mind off whatever you happen to be doing, you will lose focus, and you will more than likely fall down the rabbit hole of ruminating about whether or not you worked hard on this project.

If you were practicing mindfulness, here is how you would approach this thought differently: you would have the thought, notice how it makes you feel, recognize that it is present, and then consciously choose no to follow it down the rabbit hole. This could be done by acknowledging it mentally, saying to yourself, "I am aware that I am having this thought, but I will deal with it at another appropriate time." This is when you 'let it go.' The actual process of letting a thought go, depending on how upsetting it may be to you, may happen several days throughout the day. This is because your busy mind isn't used to letting go of subjects that could serve as a problem. But if you keep at it, the thought will eventually go away, and you will have grown that much closer to establishing mindfulness as a habit.

Here are a couple of ways of other ways in which you can start practicing mindfulness in your everyday life:

1. Take some time to notice your breathing; no matter where you are. Since the movement of your belly as it rises and falls, sensing how air moves in and out of your lungs.

2. Notice what you are doing as you are doing it by tuning into the senses involved. IF you are eating, try to notice the texture with your tongue, the way it smells through your nostrils, and linger a bit longer on it, more than you usually do.

3. Try not to give yourself some time a few times a week to simply be—and yes, when we say try doing nothing, we mean, actually nothing! Sit outside and watch the birds without your phone, sit at your desk without writing or fiddling, and allow yourself to watch your breath and your thoughts as they roll on by.

4. Start maintaining a separated belief about your thoughts; you are not fused to them; you are not defined by them. Try to imagine an animal hovering a scene, or even a plane of sorts, watching things happen as they are and simultaneously not judging or explaining them. Recognize that this is what being fully conscious is; being aware of yourself and that you are a thinking being, who can be aware of their own thinking.

5. Notice when you zone out; i.e. when you stop being present during certain habitual activities, such as driving, brushing your teeth, doing dishes, etc. When you notice this, try to be back your awareness of this activity by observing the senses again, as well as how you are breathing while partaking in the behavioral act.

The concept of mindfulness is actually quite simple, which is further complicated by Western society. It offers you a way to watch your thoughts and behavioral without judging yourself and taking a more compassionate approach. When you do this, you will find that you are significantly less stressed, because you are able to notice when you are becoming stressed. Mindfulness and meditation will be further discussed through a series of relaxation techniques in chapter 7.

2.5 Other Thinking Techniques that Diminish Stress

There are other ways that you alter the way that you think that will help you manage the stress in your life beyond mindfulness and cognitive restructuring. The next two that we are going to focus on in this book are the techniques you can apply to start thinking more rationally, and the ability to blend more positive affirmations into your daily life.

2.5.1 Becoming More Rational

What does it mean to be a rational thinker? Think of people in your life who you feel are very logical, and try to imagine how they may think. Some people are a combination of both a rational/logical thinking mind as well as a neurotic one that imagines all negative possibilities of a situation. This can make making decisions very difficult and confusing. On one hand, you are reacting to your emotions and tendency to overthink, which is the neurotic portion, while on the other, you are able to look at the situation and devise a plan that will help you solve it. But usually, the neurotic side of you takes the helm, making you question every decision and puts you into overdrive of rumination. Sound familiar?

Here is a list of ways that you can try to harness the power of being more rational, without allowing your neurotic side to take hold. These can be applied to anyone, no matter what level of rationality you may feel you are at:

1. Become Solution Oriented: Try to focus on the solutions to problems rather than wallowing in the problem itself. The key to starting to become more rational is to practice zeroing in on solutions in your everyday life, that may seem small but tend you cause you intense agitation. For example, if you can't find a parking spot, make an effort to stop yourself before you become angry by actually physically stopping the car. Sit with yourself and assess the layout of the parking lot, checking to see where the empty stops may lie. This notion of problem-solving blends with well with mindfulness, as it teaches you to focus on solving a problem rather than simply reacting to it.

2. Recognize Flaws in Your Thinking: This was previously discussed but is a practice that you should try to instill into your everyday living. We as humans constantly have to adapt, because the environment around us changes, so we must too. Situations at work may have been initially enjoyable, or at least tolerable, and have grown into an

immensely stressful, intolerable environment. This is when you must adapt.

If you are rational, you are able to recognize flaws in your thinking without feeling self-conscious or lapse into self-ridicule. Being rational means that you check your thoughts consistently and note whether or not they are realistic. To do this, you can follow the following steps:

1. Write down some of your thoughts and ask people you trust about their perspective on them. If you have a difficult time being rational in general, you may have a go-to person of whom you know is more rational, or even a therapist.
2. Admitting that you have flaws in your thinking is an incredibly adaptive tactic that will allow you to only grow and become a more contently person.
3. Doing this often will help the practice become more habitual and automatic, should a thought arise in your mind that doesn't feel reasonable.

The next chapter will focus on cognitive restructuring, a practice created by psychotherapists to help people with anxiety, mood, and anger disorders alter their thinking into more objective observation.

1. Question Your Purpose and Goals: If you are having trouble recognizing flaws in your thinking, you may have to start questioning why you do thinks. Try to analyze your goals at the moment; are you looking for a specific result? Are you being petty? Are you expectant of others? Trying to mindful of your motivations will help you notice your own biases against others and what you may believe about them, which simply isn't rational or helpful to either party. Start applying standards to your thoughts; tell yourself that they must be clear, accurate thoughts. This will help you value logical reasoning, and thus, begin to notice it in other people as well. For example, if a person you say hi to does not say hi back, you will no longer assume that they don't like you. You are now aware of other possibilities rather than assuming one; maybe they just didn't hear/see you!

2. Be Mindful of Emotions: This, of course, ties in with the concept of mindfulness and the later practice of CBT that will be discussed in this book. If you are a particularly emotional person (which you probably are if you are very stressed out), then you may rely too heavily on their presence as fact. Using the

same example as above, you may feel offended if one of your coworkers doesn't say hi to you one morning. You may feel upset or hurt, even angry. At this point, it would be best to check in with your emotions and the thoughts that they are thriving off of, such as 'wow that person must not like me' and 'I thought we were friends.' Emotions may be making the thoughts worse, or the thoughts may be making the emotions worse, or even both interchangeably. Make an effort to notice your emotions, and observe the thoughts that come off of them.

3. Keep a Journal: This was suggested earlier on, and we want to emphasize this here too! If you are trying to make an effort to observe your thinking patterns, writing it down will make it become more habitual and visual. Eventually, you won't even need the notebook, as the practice will be so ingrained in you.

4. Make Yourself More Effective: By being more rational, you will start seeing changes in your life that are positive, and most of all, the mechanisms in which you've learned to cope will stress will increase inefficiency.

2.5.2 Positive thinking: Useful vs. Toxic Positivity

Many people who may have a glass half empty mindset have been told to be more positive. Even people who are suffering from mental health disorders have been blanket-therapies by the statement, 'you just need to be more positive.' All while there are endless benefits to having a positive outlook on life and situations, there is such thing as optimism that is useful and helpful, as well as an optimism that is toxic.

Due to your life circumstances, your genetics, personality, and a vast array of other contributing factors, you may be a person who automatically looks at the bleaker side of life. For whatever reason, you have developed certain thinking habits over a lifetime that make you feel more stressed than is necessary and may be unhappier and discontented than those around you. If you feel you are this way, you've probably heard a handful of the above statements.

Maybe you have even tried and felt let down by some sweeping techniques such as forcing yourself to see 'the bright side' of everything—which eventually feels false, and ultimately, useless.

Real positive thinking doesn't mean that you stick your head in the sand and ignore all of life's problems. What it really means is to learn to look at situations more realistically, all while learning not to undermine your own ability to cope. It relies on techniques like cognitive restricting and mindfulness, that will be discussed in more detail later on.

Here are some ways you can apply a non-toxic form of positive thinking in your life:

1. Identify Areas of Change: In your notebook, make a list of the areas in your life that you feel you think most negatively about. For most people, this may be your job, a certain relationship in your life, your daily commute, or perhaps your own health. Make a hierarchy of these things, rating them from 1-whatever the number of negative things is. Start with the smallest area of your life and focus on becoming more positive about it.

2. Check Yourself: Throughout the day, stop and evaluate what you are thinking. If your thoughts are

negative, take note on how they are making you feel, even writing them down in your notebook.

3. Be Open to Humor: This doesn't mean that you are ignoring problems in your life. What it means is that you are trying to be more gentle, and lighthearted about yourself, without lapsing into deep criticism and negativity.

4. Practicing Positive-Thinking: Find specific thoughts throughout the day that you feel are particular negative. Write those down in one column in your notebook. In the next column, try to think of a positive, more realistic spin to it. You will find that the notion of being positive will open more doors for effort and development than the ones of negativity, that making assumptions of that reality being fact, and lasting forever. For example, you may be saying to yourself, "I am not going to get any better at this." If you think this way, of course, you are going to stop trying. If you change thought to "I will try again tomorrow" or even "no everyone is good at everything, but I want to try to learn more about this", you will feel better at making more effort and no longer determining that you are not good enough for a certain task.

This chapter focused on general ways that you can begin reflecting and thinking about how you think, which greatly affects your stress levels. The next chapter will focus on what happens when you do not deal with your negative thinking patterns, along with the external and internal events that cause you to feel overwhelmed with stress.

Chapter 3: How Stress Develops into Mental Health Disorders and How to Overcome Them (Depression, Anxiety, and Anger Issues)

Stress is an emotion that manifests itself psychologically and physically and when not dealt with in a healthy manner, can evolve into something much more pervasive and difficult to hand: mental health disorders. Mental health disorders can be defined as extreme experiences of stress, negative moods such as sadness, indifference, anger, and anxiety, over periods of months, and even years. Mental health issue develops for a variety of reasons: the environment in which you were raised, your particular genetics, your coping mechanisms, your external and internal stressors, and cultural norms. They can arise at any point in a person's life, but generally coming into full swing around young adulthood or after the experience of trauma. In relation to this book, they can be caused in intense, chronic stress, and/or stress can be a symptom experienced. This chapter is going to dive deeper into the CBT notion of cognitive distortions and will teach you how to restructure your thinking habits in relation to your particular disorder. Should you feel you do not fall under the category of any of the following disorders, you will still benefit from the practice of restructuring as a whole, because it focuses on helping people think more rationally.

1. Anxiety Disorders: The experience of consistent physical and psychological symptoms of anxiety such as racing heart, rapid thoughts, sweating shaking, and a seemingly uncontrolled fear of a particular stimulus. Some people with anxiety disorders have a specific phobia, such as social phobia, or follow obsessive rituals in order to neutralize an intrusive thought that makes them anxious (obsessive-compulsive disorder). People who have a generalized anxiety disorder (GAD) are constantly plagued by worry about their jobs, what their friends think of them, natural disasters, possible accidents, or an abundant or any other negative outcomes.

2. Mood Disorders (Depression): Mood disorders can range from bipolar disorder (a shifting from an intense high called mania, to an intense low called

depression), to the experience of major depression. This section is going to focus mainly on the depressive symptoms, which involve a feeling of indifference, disinterest in life's activities, lack of motivation, and possible suicidal ideation and thoughts.

3. Anger Disorders: People with anger issue are sometimes diagnosed with the intermittent explosive disorder (IED) or other impulse-control issues. This chapter is going to focus on the experience of anger and how it can be experienced and controlled in a healthier manner.

3.1 Cognitive Distortions and Anxiety

1. Catastrophizing: This is the least surprising cognitive distortion that dominates anyone who has experienced any form of anxiety throughout their lives. This is when the worst possible conclusion is assumed, based on very little or even zero evidence to the contrary. A person may have anxiety about driving and assumes that whenever they get into the front seat that they are doomed to accidentally run over someone. It is literally thinking that a disaster is going to occur, no matter how large or small, in

every situation. One is situational, like that of deriving or going to a party and assuming no one is going to like you, while the second projects into the future and anticipates that everything is going to go wrong. It is a cycle that is difficult to break, which is why initially noticing when these thoughts are occurring is all that this chapter will ask of you. If you feel your catastrophes, write down what your thoughts are exactly, and how emotions and behavior that followed were in line with it. Trying a single thought that is the opposite of what you are assuming, and see how it makes you feel (write this down too).

2. Polarized thinking: This is when a person with anxiety only thinks in terms of overly good, overly bad, in a pure level that includes no shades of grey. This is often a surefire way of getting your hopes destroyed because the weight of the importance of the outcome becomes too heavy to even bare. If you get into college, your life will be great forever. If you do not, then your life is over. This is a detriment way of thinking, but life has naturally not entirely bad, nor entirely good. It is an unrealistic way of thinking. If you feel you do this, write down the thoughts you are having that are a direct reference

to your polarized thinking. Write down the two outcomes of being entirely bad or entire good. Then down the middle, try to think of the way you would learn to cope if the situation did not entirely go your way. Realize that life can go, and a summary of it does not depend upon the success of a single event.

3. Filtering: People with anxiety are great at only nothing the supposed negative of any event, compliment, occurrence, etc., that happens in their lives. The simplest example would be the student that gets an A on an assignment, and while everyone else praises them, they wonder what they could have done wrong to not have received an A-plus. If there was a party, and a person accidentally spilled their drink on the kitchen counter, but the rest of the party was fun and enjoyable, the person may be focusing entirely on their single event of accidentally spilling a drink. These cognitive distortions all play upon each other, which is why they function so well for such a long time. Next time you feel you are focusing too hard on a negative event, try to focus on the rest of the situation that may have been positive. Begin practicing this mentally the time for minimizing arrives in your life.

4. Personalization: This is when people with anxiety take everything that happens in their external world to have to do with them. This makes you feel responsible for every person you know the mood, comfort, etc. Personalization also leads to comparing yourself to others and deeming yourself valuable only in comparison to them. You may compare yourself to someone else intelligence, attractiveness, skill level, etc. Try to take note when you feel you have done something to upset someone, or are comprising yourself to others. Note it makes you feel. Try to use another thought that realizes you are not responsible for the mood of others and see how you feel then.

5. Overgeneralization: This happens to toe people with anxiety often because absolute words are used, such as 'always' and 'never.' These assumptions may be based upon negative experiences of the past. For example, a person who has anxiety that was just dumped by their significant other, they make the vast overgeneralization that no one will ever love me again'. These statements are not facts at all. Overgeneralization also assumes what other people are feeling and thinking, without having had any exchange or understanding as such. You may also

make generalizations about having to go to a party, deeming that you 'never' have fun and react around this statement as if it is a fact. If you feel you do this, try to remember to write down either the statements or thoughts that include absolutes like 'never' or 'always.' Then when you have a moment, try to think about this in a literal; do you actually always have a bad time when you go to parties? Or is it because you anticipate that you won't have fun that fun is not had? Look at these statements and challenge them with facts.

6. Attribution Errors: This is similar to overgeneralization. This is when we assume we know everything there is to know about a person's motivation for their behavior and believe that the actions may have been deliberate in their results. This distortion does not take into consideration facts or relayed realities from another person. You simply are assuming that what another person may have done is done for reasons that have to do with you. This is when we judge people based on the behavior rather than investigating their intent. An example of this with anxiety is when you try to say hello to a friend, and they rush past you inside of replying. You assume that the person was rude and that it

was directly done to you and have you be hurt. To start challenging these thoughts, think about how well you know your friend, how they aren't likely to often act this way, and what may have been going through their mind that may have nothing to do with you.

3.2 Cognitive Distortions and Depression

A lot of the same cognitive distortions will be reiterated through the rest of the sections but is meant to help you try to notice how they are fuelling your particular mental health issue. Examples directly relating to depression will be focused on in this section.

1. Polarized thinking: You have applied for a job that you really wanted, but you did not get it. Because of this, you feel like a failure and that you will never get the job that you truly desire.
2. Overgeneralization: You may have tried to go out and meet new people, but you had no luck, therefore, to you, all people are unkind and judgmental. This may be due to a few experienced that are isolated.

3. Filtering: A good friend may have come to visit you, but they brought you the wrong donuts that they promised you for. You focus on that one detail, rather than the fact that a good friend tried to go out of their way to comfort you.

4. Disqualifying the positive: A person with depression would be quick to brush away compliments about their looks, talent, kindness, etc. If they achieve something positive in their lives, liking getting a drivers license or a new job, they shrug it off as not a big deal and focus on what they perceive as negative in the situation.

5. Jumping to conclusions: They can occur easily in relationships with people with depression. When dating, if a person does not arrive on time, or reply to a text very quickly, then they must dislike them or have rejected them. There is a belief that perhaps they did something wrong rather than recognizing that there are influences far beyond their control.

6. Magnifying and Minimization: The ability to make something negative larger and something positive smaller is a common occurrence amongst those with depression. A person with depression may have managed to make a delicious meal for the company one night and is praised for their skill and effort. The

person brushes this off, saying that the good was easy to make anyway.

7. Emotional Reasoning: This is when a person with depression will use their emotions as facts to inspire their behavior. For example, a person may look at their untidy room or house, and feel that it is pointless and hopeless to begin cleaning it now. They are using their own reaction to the mess as evidence that it will never get better, so why try again?

8. Should Statements: These are statements we make to ourselves either about ourselves or about others. This is when you place another person's behavior on a pedestal based on nothing but their career, their perceived skill, etc. You may also have used this distortion to apply to yourself and how you compare yourself to others; 'I should be married with kids by this age"; "I should be making more money," etc.

9. Labeling and Mislabeling: This occurs when a person puts an entire arcing label on something that relates to their behavior or overall life status. For example, if a person cheats on their diet, then they are 'lazy and useless.' If a person misses a single class or single day of work, then they label themselves as a 'failure.'

10. Personalization: A person may think that it is their fault that their child is not doing well in school. Their partner may often be in a bad mood, and they assume that it is because of them.

3.3 Cognitive Distortions and Anger Management

1. Blaming: These are the most self-destructive cognitive distortions that greatly encourages the continued sensation of anger. This belief relies on the interpretation that other people are trying to do bad things to you, and generally on purpose. Blaming can help someone feel better sometimes because it removes the responsibility of the feeling and situation from you to someone else. You have given up the power to change the situation, which makes it harder to want to change along the line.

2. Catastrophizing: This distortion is common amongst all of the disorders discussed in this book. The continued belief that everything is going to go wrong, and not being surprised when it doesn't or you interpret it as not going well, fuels your right to express anger in whatever format you deem fit. You can easily become angry when things seem to be

absolutely terrible because it allows you to once again, express yourself outwardly instead of looking inward on how you can change your situation.

3. Inflammatory Global Labelling: This occurs when a person is angry through name-calling, whether it be direct or with others the person trusts. This is when a person makes a sweeping judgment about the behavior of others, reducing them to something worthless and inhuman. This only fuels the anger more because you are no longer discussing a person or attempting to understand their motivations.

4. Mis attributions: This is when a person is hurt or irritated by another's behavior, and makes the assumption that they committed this behavior on purpose in order to injure you. Believing this will only make you angrier because it is unacceptable for another person to have an ill-will toward you.

5. Overgeneralization: Absolute words like 'never' and 'always' are used with people who have problems with anger too. This makes a person only look for and notice the negative behaviors of others and furthers the belief that they are not good. Other words that are used to label others such as 'nobody' and 'everyone' only expect the worse out of every person you may encounter.

6. Demanding and Commanding: This is when a person turns their own personal preferences into demands. This is when a person with anger issues believes that their needs and values must align directly with others, and when they don't, it is obviously the fault of the other person (in their eyes.)

Most of these cognitive distortions will go hand-in-hand with low self-esteem, relationship insecurity, lack of exercise, accompanying medical conditions, incorrect medication intake, etc. The symptoms described previously in the chapters that detailed the mental health issues are very real. The theories and practices of CBT believe in the application of these tools and assert the belief that cognitive distortions are mere portions of what makes worse distortions the symptoms of depression, anxiety, and anger issues.

3.4 Cognitive Restructuring: Anxiety

This section will explore specific exercises that you can apply in order to begin challenging the cognitive distortions that are more than likely making your anxiety worse. Other chapters in the book will explore other tools to add to your toolkit, depending on what form of anxiety you may be experiencing. There are many ways that one can combat anxiety and learn to live a more fulfilling life, and the advice in this section is only some of them.

If you feel you are suffering from anxiety or a particular kind of anxiety disorder, read on. First, take a glance at your notebook where you wrote down your experience of mood, thoughts, and behavior for a week. In the next week, you observed your cognitive distortions and highlighted the ones that you feel were the most intrusive in your life. If you feel you express yourself through the examples described previously in this chapter, feel free to highlight that section or write it down next to your cognitive distortion list. Now, we will focus on ways you can challenge these distortions. Other advice in relation to each cognitive distortion will also be shared.

3.5 The Importance of Thought Records with Anxiety

There following sheet is generalized anxiety thought the record that challenges cognitive distortions. There are many kinds of thought records that exist depending on the kind of disorder and cognitive distortions you are choosing to challenge. The following is a sample sheet taken from GetSelfHelp:

Thought Record Sheet – 7 column

Situation / Trigger	Feelings Emotions – (Rate 0 – 100%) Body sensations	Unhelpful Thoughts / Images	Facts that support the unhelpful thought	Facts that provide evidence against the unhelpful thought	Alternative, more realistic and balanced perspective	Outcome Re-rate emotion
What happened? Where? When? Who with? How?	What emotion did I feel at that time? What else? How intense was it? What did I notice in my body? Where did I feel it?	What went through my mind? What disturbed me? What did those thoughts/images/memories mean to me, or say about me or the situation? What am I responding to? What 'button' is this pressing for me? What would be the worst thing about that, or that could happen?	What are the facts? What facts do I have that the unhelpful thought/s are totally true?	What facts do I have that the unhelpful thought/s are NOT totally true? Is it possible that this is opinion, rather than fact? What have others said about this?	STOP!! Take a breath... What would someone else say about this situation? What's the bigger picture? Is there another way of seeing it? What advice would I give someone else? Is my reaction in proportion to the actual event? Is this really as important as it seems?	What am I feeling now? (0-100%) What could I do differently? What would be more effective? Do what works! Act wisely. What will be most helpful for me or the situation? What will the consequences be?

We will go through each section, using various examples of thoughts and feelings felt by individuals with general anxiety or social anxiety. (These are two of the most common disorders that apply this thought sheet in relation to anxiety) These records can be done in anticipation of an occurrence or done while looking back on something that has occurred in the past. It is better to use an example of something that is likely to happen so you can learn to practice cognitive restructuring at the moment.

1. Column 1: Situation/Trigger: You may have to pay for something at a store, but have never used a debit card before. The thought about having to do this triggers anxiety in you. A description of that trigger will be written into the first column.

2. Column 2: Feelings/Emotions: Rate your anxiety level from 0-100. Describe how the emotions are felt in your body. In this example, your pulse may be racing, your palms sweaty, are breathing rapidly, etc. Try to rate each bodily experience from the intensity of 0-100, 100 being the worst anxiety you have experienced.

3. Column 3: Unhelpful Thoughts/Images: This is where the cognitive distortions come into play. In this situation, a flood of thoughts probably arrived in unison with the physical sensations. Thoughts such as 'what if I look stupid' 'what if they all judge me for not knowing how to use a debit card?'. Memories of similar situations may come back too. Try to write down as many of the thoughts as you can in this section.

4. Column 4: Facts that Support the Unhelpful Thought: For a person with social anxiety, feeling embarrassed, or looking stupid is one of their greatest fears. Avoidance of situations that stimulate

this anxiety is generally how they try to function. This section tries to focus on facts that people may think you're stupid, may judge you for the expression of your anxiety, etc. Make sure you only write actual facts here, not the assumptions of others' thoughts, the integration of behavior, etc. When you begin, you may feel a certain look someone gives you in line, or the cashier means that they are judging something about you. This is, though, not a fact. If there was an experience in the past where a person directly pointed at you and said out loud, "wow, you don't know what to use a debit card? You're an idiot," then that would be a fact. If there are people in line who seem to be a rush, and this is supporting your unhelpful thought, then write that down. Soon the distinction between fact and your cognitive distortions will become easier to notice.

5. Column 5: Facts that Provide Evidence Against the Unhelpful Thought: In this situation, there is an abundant amount of information that goes against the unhelpful thought. For example, no one has ever pointed at you and told you were stupid, too anxious, etc. You can note how distracted the cashier is, how other people take a long time

figuring out their debit and credit cards, etc. Anything that is a fact outside of you that is against the interpretation that others think you are stupid is what you will write down here.

6. Column 6: There are many questions in this section at the bottom of the column that can aid you in exploring how you can reframe your unhelpful thought, to one that is more realistic. Try to ask yourself how others would view the situation, if you are making it larger than it needs to be, and if this interaction were as it important as it feels? After asking yourself these questions, try to reframe the initial anxious thoughts that you wrote down in the third column. In this example, instead of wondering if people will think you're stupid or too anxious, try to think: 'it is okay if I don't know how to use the machine, a lot of people don't/it is ok if someone sees my anxiety, because a lot of people have anxiety about new things too.'

7. Column 7: Finally, re-rate how you are feeling after you have re-framed the thought around the reality of the situation. Do this between 0-100 again? Write down what your body is feeling too, in relation to what you have previously written.

Now since you have used this thought record once, think of the top 5 most anxiety triggering situations that have either already occurred in your life or that you are anticipating. Write out the thought record for each one, re-framing your way of thinking. If the situation were to actually occur, try to remember as many details as you can so you write out another thought record, and how you tried to apply a reframed thought. If you did not use the new thought, or you felt your anxiety did not go down as much as you hoped, re-read the thought record you previously wrote when you were not in the situation. As previously said, it is going to take some time for this practice to become a habit. Do not expect yourself to be free of anxiety the first time you try to re-frame your thinking. Other sections of this book will focus more on the behavioral portion of CBT and how it can help you learn better on how to cope with your anxiety symptoms and methods of thinking.

Examples of rating your top 5 situational triggers of anxiety could be as follows:

<u>For Social Anxiety:</u>
5. Saying hello to a crossing guard
4. Answering the phone

3. Ordering food in a restaurant

2. Using a debit/credit card

1. Returning an item to a store.

<u>For Generalized Anxiety:</u>

5. Riding in a car

4. Watching the news

3. Disagreeing with a family member

2. Visiting a cemetery

1. Going to job interviews

Rate your anxiety triggering events from the highest number, act as the less anxiety triggering event, to the lowest, number 1 acting as the most anxiety-causing event. The particular triggers will different to each person, depending on what makes them anxious most and what their anxiety disorder may be diagnosed as. A person may have a specific phobia, OCD, PTSD, etc., so their triggers will be different from the examples above.

Keep your top 5 list in mind in your notebook as they will come in handy in the next chapter.

3.6 Restructuring Depression

Challenging thoughts as it relates to depressive symptoms is very similar to that of a person with anxiety. Thoughts are believed to be an incredibly powerful influencer for those who have suffered from depression for a long time. Very often, a person is so deep and set in their ways of feeling depressed; their behavior coordinates along with their thoughts, which only furthers the cycle of their negative mood. CBT attempts to infiltrate this cycle by asking the sufferer to observe their thoughts and realize that they are not as realistic as their accompanying emotions believe them to be.

The previously mentioned thought record is recommended for the use of those who are depressed as well. It looks at feelings, physical sensations, behaviors, and thoughts as they work together in a single experience of depression. Another example will be explained here as it relates to an individual with depression as opposed to someone with anxiety.

Since you have previously observed your mood, you more than likely have noticed common themes in what will trigger a more downward mood or time of day, or whether or not you had taken medication, exercised, etc. For some people, their depression is worse in the morning, and a low mood is triggered by an argument, or in relation to work, or ruminating about a past relationship. These are only a few examples.

It may be harder for someone who has been stuck in a depressive state for a long time to take note of when their mood is at its worst vs. when it is not as bad. This is why it is important to follow through on the first steps of this book, that focuses entirely on the observation of mood.

In this example, I will use the example of job seeking. This is a very common trigger for many people suffering from depression. Perhaps they were just let go, or are having a difficult time finding work. First, you will write the date and time. Next, you describe the situation. In this case, it could be the mere fact that you have not heard back from any jobs that you applied to, or just received an email that rejected you from a certain role.

This may cause you to feel depressed. In this section, describe the physical sensations you feel that accompany these automatic thoughts. Some people feel a drop in their stomach, tear-eyed, nausea, weak limbs, or the desire to lie down and not move all day. Some automatic thoughts that may arise are:

"I am never going to get a job."
"No one wants to hire me because I'm useless."
"I've wasted my life and have amounted to nothing."

In the next section, you will describe the emotions the best way you can that accompanied the thoughts. The descriptions can be as general as sad, mad, and frustrated. If you feel the need to go into more detail than feel free to do so. Rate the emotions in intensity from 0-100.

Now, take a look back in your notebook at the cognitive distortions you identified as being your most common go-to's. In this example, the person is experiencing all-or-nothing thinking, overgeneralization, and catastrophizing. Write down the styles you feel your thoughts are reflecting in this section of the table. Then, ask yourself the questions that are written at the bottom of the table. This asks you to search for evidence that each thought is true, and then untrue.

You may need extra paper for this section. Do this for each thought? In this example, evidence searching could appear as follows, as well as a rating from 0-100 on how much you actually believe the thought:

Thought 1: "I am never going to get a job"
- Evidence of truth: None.
- Evidence of Lies: I cannot predict the future. I have also had jobs in the past, so this statement just isn't fact.

Thought 2: "No one wants to hire me because I'm useless"
- Evidence of truth: Email received from employer applied to.
- Evidence of Lies: 'No one' is a very sweeping statement. I have not met everyone in the world who is hiring someone. No one has ever called me useless before.

Thought 3: "I've wanted my life and have amounted to nothing"
- Evidence of Truth: Do not have a lot of savings, still live at home, do not have a partner.

- Evidence of Lies: My life is not over yet. I am only X age. I have a roof over my head. I have held jobs in the past and have been successful and thrived in them.

Now, you will re-assess your automatic thoughts and gauge how much you actually believe these statements that you have made, using the same rating system. Observe your emotions and rate their level of intensity.

Try to apply this automatic thought record response to your top five most mistaken beliefs that contribute to your depression. Link them once again to cognitive distortions, and go over this workout in relation to each of them. This may be something that is more difficult to do, depending upon the intensity of your depression. Goal-seeking for those with depression is also highly important for recovery and will be discussed in a later chapter. For now, try to write out an automatic thought record once a day this week, or once every other day. Discuss it with your partner, or someone you trust if it feels overwhelming.

3.7 The ABCDE Model of Cognitive Restructuring

The above model is an example of how events, behaviors, emotions, and beliefs all work together in conjunction and allow a certain mental health issue to thrive. Recognizing the link between them has been proven to help those suffering from depression. This form of restructuring can be recalled as:

A= Activating Event: An event that leads to the thoughts that led to emotional or behavioral issues.

B= Belief or thought about the event.

C= Consequences: Behaviors and feelings that come out due to the thoughts about the activating event.)

D= Deciphering: Recognizing and understanding, then finally defeating automatic negative thoughts.

E= Evidenced based positive thought development.

The ABCDE Model can also be used as a thought record for those with depression. Each letter would represent a single column that describes the particular event, the reaction to the event, and the re-framing that occurring to begin looking differently at the event. It can be presented as follows:

A: Situation, thought, or physical sensation; do your best to be specific. Describe the 'who, what, where, when.' With an example of a person with depression, the activating event may be the thought like: "I am not attractive enough to find a partner." This thought could have been triggered by rejection, or a perceived reject, or even come out of the nowhere once the discussion or thought of dating arose around them.

B: Listing all of the thoughts you had about A; then describe which thought caused the most depressing feeling. Then rate how true you think this thought is. For example, a thought that may accompany the triggering event A (which is also thought; thoughts can be triggering events too); maybe "yeah, I'll probably just end up dying alone.' From a rating from 1-10, this may have caused this person the intensity of depression at a 9.

C: This section describes the accompanying actions and feelings. Describe specifically how you feel. Identify which feeling directly tied to your activating event (A). Rate how strong that feeling is again on a scale of 1-10. Then write down the behaviors/reactions you made to your activating event. Then try to observe and see which behavior is most associated with the activating event. In our example, it may read as follows; "I feel like a complete loser. I feel ugly and unwanted. This feeling is at the intensity of an 8. I was lying in bed and swiping on tinder and decided to delete the app entirely. I tried to sleep but ended up crying for a while."

D: Try to find which thought caused the most depressed and unpleasant feeling. Locate the cognitive distortion this thought falls under. Note if the thought is true if it is a productive way to think, what others may think about your thoughts and reaction. Access if your behaviors are rational. Explore yourself and question if you would be having this thought if you weren't distressed? An example of a reply to this section would be: "The thought that bothers me to the most is the one that predicts that I will 'die alone.' This is an overgeneralization. The thought isn't necessarily true because my life is not over yet. This does not help me feel better about myself. An observer may think that I am too hard on myself and says that dating comes in phases of life. My action of deleting the app is not rational because it may help me actually meet someone when I am ready. If I wasn't so stressed about being single, I probably wouldn't be having this thought."

E: The final section applies what cognitive behavior therapy is mainly known for; the search for evidence that supports, and evidence that does not support mistaken beliefs and thoughts. It asks for you to replace the most powerful negative thought with a more rational, healthy thought. If you have control over the issue, try to think of proactive ways you can make yourself feel better. It is recommended that you do guide breathing or relaxation exercise (which will be discussed later). Finally, reevaluate how you are feeling, between 1-10, and your thoughts, between 1-10, depending on how rational they are. Our example may state: "A thought that is more positive to replace the thought of 'I am just going to die alone' is 'Maybe I will find someone who best suits me one day, but it is okay if I don't too.' Actions I could take would be ones that invest me in my own hobbies rather than into someone else. If I wanted to date, I can try to go out more often, or let my friends know that I am open to dating. I re-evaluated my feelings on the intensity, and they are at a 5; the level of rationality has also gone down to a 5."

Thought records and cognitive restructuring, such as the one mentioned above, are not meant to permanently rid you of thoughts that bother you. They are merely meant as a practice to help you re-learn how to think and behave in healthier, and beneficial ways. Not all thought records will work for everyone, so feel free to try a few of them. No, not to be hard on yourself should your depressive mood not instantly live. It is not meant to instantly. It will be constantly emphasized in this book how important practice as, like any sport, it takes time to be mastered.

3.7 Cognitive Restructuring and Anger

Anger issues and cognitive restructuring are slightly different from the practice recommended for those who suffer from anxiety issues or depression. Anger is an emotion that rises and falls fast and is quickly associated with negative behavior expressed externally. What cognitive restructuring with anger issues focuses on is the ability to notice the feeling of anger rising, whether it be mentally or within the experience of physical sensations, to re-frame your perceive, and to choose to respond to the situation in a more practice manner. Like all of the skills practiced in this book, learning to do all of those things in a single snap is going to take time. That is why it is important to learn about the physical sensations, the triggers, and the associated thoughts and beliefs that accompany your intense expression of anger.

The Association for Behavioral and Cognitive Therapies writes about the important factors that can help someone apply the techniques of CBT when they feel their anger is too overwhelming:

1. Enhanced Personal Awareness: This notion was previously discussed in the section that explored cognitive distortions that are particular to having anger issues. A lot of people who overreact to situations, such as traffic jams and missing a train, are not aware that their anger may be disproportional. The first portion of this book asked you to observe your moods, thoughts, and behaviors then asked you to identify cognitive distortions. If you have done so, then you should be more aware of what, how, and why certain things make you so angry.

2. **Anger Disruption by Avoidance and Removal:** As mentioned, the triggering of anger is often situational, unless the individual is ruminating about a past event that may have caused the anger. This technique focuses on removing you, whether it be mentally or physically, from the situation that is causing the anger. This may be a wise tactic for the early days of your CBT therapy. Doing this will allow you to move away from the trigger and gather the information necessary if a reply is needed. Perhaps you can use other forms of communication that you feel you can have more control over for now, such as an email or a letter of reply. Going away will allow your anger to dissipate, so you can reply differently later. Finding a productive task to do instead of engaging in angry behavior is also another technique that has been recommending by those who practice CBT. This can be something as simple as taking a shower, cooking, or doing laundry. This again, allows you to calm down. With this skill plus self-awareness, you will begin to notice even more what may set you off.

3. **Relaxation Coping Skills:** Learning breathing techniques and relaxation skills are going to be a vital practice to master for those who suffer from

anger management issues. Once you are aware of what triggers you, you can begin noticing your physical reactions to the anger and apply these techniques in order to lower this sensation. Visualization of an angry event and calming your anger down is a good way to practice before external stimuli have a chance to trigger you. Practicing these skills at home will help you feel a stronger sense of control for when you begin to feel the anger rising in your day-to-day life. The particulars of these techniques will be described in chapter seven.

4. Attitude and Cognitive Change: This section also explores the attitudes that have been contributing to the experience of intensely angry moods. As previously mentioned, people with anger issues often use words such as should ought, have to, etc. They expect other people's behavior to align with their own preferences. Once you are able to identify these thoughts and recognize that they are not rational and do not help you feel better about yourself. This perspective also allows you to begin accepting the fact that you cannot control another person's behaviors. This will involve similar thought records as those recommended for those with

anxiety and depression. You will identify the thought and cognitive distortion that connects you to the feeling of anger. There are other ways that a therapist may apply this exploration, such as through:

a) Role-playing: Playing out a situation that may have already occurred, or the person is anticipating. You will learn relaxation techniques and will practice re-framing at the moment that will help you learn to calm down faster.

b) Self-monitoring: This is where a therapist may teach a person to observe the level of anger rising inside you before it comes out to express itself.

The overall goal here is to identify anger triggering thoughts and then to replace them with thoughts that are more reasonable. For example, the anger thought of "he should have known that I'd be hungry when I got home from work," which is thought in reaction to coming home and finding little food in the fridge, with that thought that states "maybe he forgot. He could have had a hard day as well. Besides, no one is perfect."

1. Acceptance and Forgiveness: This notion recognizes the natural faults that exist in humans as human beings. There are always going to be events and occurrences that are beyond your control, no matter how many times you try to re-frame a situation. A flight may be delayed due to weather; a child may spill drinks, spouses sometimes forget to replace the milk once they've finished it. Just like you, no one is always going to act perfectly. Thinking that other people always act to hurt you, or that they should have behaved differently, is hypocritical. Learning to understand that oftentimes the behavior of others has little if anything to do with us helps you shift your point of view into that of a more realistic one. This will help you notice more often when you are blaming others, getting annoyed at them for not being perfect, or yelling at them for a behavior that was a natural human mistake.

2. Skill Enhancement: Along with observations, thoughts, and mistaken beliefs, adding problem-solving skills to your toolkit may help you deal with conflict in a healthier manner once it arrives upon the scene again. Disagreements and arguments are still going to happen between people who care about

each other, coworkers, strangers, etc. Signing up for a class that helps you better communicate with your spouse is a great way to re-connect and to learn more about how you can get your feelings across to them. Sometimes people use intense anger as an outlet because they do not possess the appropriate skills that are necessary to help communicate about a particular issue. Assertiveness training is a popular choice for a lot of people with anger issues; lack of assertiveness commonly shows its face as intense anger.

Just like in the previous two chapters, try to take note of your top five issues that make you the angriest. Rate them from 1-5. This is going to be important for the next chapter that will discuss visualization.

This chapter has mainly focused on the cognitive portion of CBT. Though it was suggested that you observe your behaviors, whether it be situational or looking into the past, the time to take action in the behavioral section of CBT is now. If you do not feel ready to take on the next chapter, go over this past one a few more times.

3.8 Anxiety: Exposure and Response Prevention

Exposure and response prevention, or ERP, is a CBT technique created particularly for those who suffer from obsessive-compulsive disorder. Since those who suffer from OCD possess a very identifiable cycle of their suffering, the experience of both obsessions and compulsions, ERP seeks to expose the person particular fear and to re-train their brain not to react with a compulsion. For example, a person who suffers from the desire to check their stove five times before they leave the house may be asked to slowly diminish the number of times they check, eventually falling to once and then leaving the house. The compulsion is a reaction that is meant to take away the anxiety that accompanies the experience of the thought, so the notion of not partaking in the compulsion will inherently cause a lot of anxiety. The goal of ERP is to show you that you can cope with the anxiety that arrives when the compulsion is resisted.

The best way to explain the importance and usefulness of ERP is to apply the metaphor of a swimming pool. If you jump directly into the deep end of a pool, it is more than likely going to bed very cold. Your body goes into shock because of the abrupt temperature change. At first, your body is in panic body, the experience of the cold takes time to sink into your skin so the rest of your organs can adjust to the change of environment. Eventually, though, you will no longer feel that shock, nor the same intense cold as when you first jumped in. ERP is likened to this adjustment of sensations; it teaches the person with OCD that they are more than capable of experiencing the physical and psychological sensations that come along with their anxiety. Initially, the experience of it will feel intense, and it will be hard not to want to escape the sensation by partaking in a compulsion. But the body cannot stay anxious forever. By observing how the symptoms of the body's reaction, anxiety slowly diminish, you realize that you are more in control that your OCD wants to convince you of. The feared result of not participating in the compulsion will more than likely not happen.

The metaphor, of course, makes it all sound easier said than done. Specific obsessions may have built up over years of anxiety, so facing down something that has caused you such agony is not something that is going to be a walk in the par. But know that the fact that you are reading this book means that you are brave.

ERP does not ask you to jump into the deep end. It asks you to make a list of your most anxiety-producing obsessions, rank them from 1-10, and to slowly begin from the bottom all the way to the top of your hierarchy to the most anxiety-inducing obsession. Exposure tasks may also be divided up into smaller tasks, so the intensity of not performing compulsions doesn't feel so debilitating.

First, start by making a list of your most common obsessions and their accompanying compulsions. Try to begin with your most anxiety-producing obsession, and then go down from there. To make the process easier for yourself, it is better to start at the bottom of your list, near the least anxiety-producing obsession: (example worksheet presented by Therapist Aid).

Every person with OCD has different obsessions and compulsions. Try to think of at least ten different obsessions that may be a part of your OCD experience. Begin by choosing number 10. An obsession of a fear which is afraid to be around knives will be used to further display how this technique will work.

Let's say that a fear of being around knives, using knives, etc., is your number 10 most anxiety-producing obsession. The compulsion that you engage in order to not feel anxiety is to avoid going into the kitchen, eating alone without the use of knives, and trying not to look at them if you absolutely have to be around them. The thoughts that accompany this obsession revolve around death, the images that it connotes, and your fear that you may have the urge the use the knife on someone you love, or yourself.

The next step is to begin participating in the exposure of the triggering stimulus. For this obsession, and any other obsession that may be bothering you, we will divide up the exposure into smaller steps. You can do this yourself too. Start small, and gradually, make a list of steps that will expose you to your fear stimulus on a defending scale. Rate the level of fear from 0-100. Your step chart may look something like this:

Exposure Fear Level (0-100)

- Take a single step into the kitchen in the direction of the knives: 30
- Stand in front of the knives for thirty seconds: 50-70
- Touch a knife, perhaps hold it for thirty seconds to a minute: 70
- Use the knife to cut up a small fruit or vegetable: 80-90
- Use the knife to consume an entire meal that requires a knife: 100

Even if the steps you initially create are too much of a jump, don't feel bad. If an exposure session has to be divided up into smaller pieces in order to help you endure it, there is nothing wrong with that. Once you have made a list that you find suitable, you can start recording your responses to the exposure session. You can use your notebook to write down the physical sensations you experienced, as well as the level of anxiety you felt while enduring the exposure. Rate your level of anxiety from 1-100. Make a note of how long you feel it took for your anxiety to lower to at least a 30 or 40.

If you consistently expose yourself to this step, the faster your anxiety will come down. Once you have experienced 30 or lower-level anxiety at least three times, you can move onto the next step in your exposure list.

The rating of 0-100 is sometimes called SUDS and stands for subjective units of distress. This rating system is also used during other forms of anxiety exposure.

It is recommended that you participate in exposure every day until the SUDS has lowered to a 30 or has completely diminished. Do not jump too fast onto the next step in exposure, or onto the next obsession on your list. This can cause a setback and make you feel overwhelmed. CBT that is effective will lead to what is called habituation; your mind and body have become used to the presence of the obsession (whether it is a thought or external stimuli) and you have learned that nothing bad will happen if you do not engage in your compulsions.

Exposure and response prevention is a CBT technique that longs to break two types of associations occurring in OCD. There are:

1. The association between sensations of stress and discomfort around certain thoughts, objects, etc. (the obsession and the anxiety felt).
2. The association between carrying out compulsive behavior that will decrease the distress.

3.9 Coping with Physical and Psychological Sensations During Exposure: Fear of 'Losing Control'

One of the hardest parts of exposure therapy is that it involves intentionally causing anxiety. The majority of the time, the ways in which people cope with their anxiety is to avoid it altogether. The initial experience of putting yourself into an anxiety-inducing situation will feel like the worst anxiety you have ever felt. There are the physical sensations of anxiety; the shaking, the racing pulse, the sweating, take make you feel like you cannot focus and convince you that you are not in control. This mix in with psychological sensations, such as thoughts that accompany the feeling of fear. Some accompanying thoughts might include the fear of going crazy, losing control, and the basic assumption that you will not be able to cope with the feelings you are having.

The entire point of ERP is to allow you to learn that these thoughts are not true. That goes along with the previously identified cognitive distortions you noted in the previous chapter. In order to learn to cope with the associated physical and psychological sensations during exposure, you must make sure you are making a hierarchy that is reasonable, and are doing it on a daily basis. If you are seeing a therapist, you can possibly begin doing it with them. Or you can do it with a person you trust. If the concept of putting yourself in vivo (meaning 'live' or 'in-person') exposure, you can begin with your first step via imagined exposure. The process is still the same, and you must do your best to allow the anxiety to fall from its increased state to a 30 or 0 before stopping the exposure.

3.10 Safety Behaviors and Disconnecting

One of the most common blocks to progress and recoveries while apply ERP is the application of safety behaviors and disconnecting. Safety behaviors may seem similar to rituals. In our knife obsession example, instead of staring at the knife and allowing their obsessive thoughts to flow, a person may be staring at the counter instead, choosing to think of anything else besides the obsession. Of course, the anxiety is going to dissipate, because you have found a distraction. Perhaps this is even a ritual the person participates in order to rid themselves of their anxiety. Disconnecting is very similar, in the sense that it avoids feeling the sensations of anxiety. Another example could have a person holding the knife in their hand, or using the knife while eating an entire meal, but chose to think about something else in order to avoid the thoughts that disturb them the most.

These activities are natural because you have spent a lot of your life trying to avoid the horrible feeling some of those thoughts are giving you. You once believed that you could not cope with them. But ERP therapy conducted all over the world have said otherwise; habituation is a science, and a guarantee that will occur once you allow yourself to feel all of the sensations that anxiety is going to throw at you.

Once you make your list, try to consult with someone you know or someone who you trust who can be present for your self-ERP sessions. Setbacks will happen, such as the compulsive engagement in rituals, and the elevation of anxiety the second or third day you choose to tackle an exposure step. Do not be discouraged by this. This only means that you are trying something different, and your body is reacting. Think about the slow steps of getting into a pool. That is, you; getting used to the notion of anxious thoughts and feelings, and how little control they have over you.

3.11 Dealing with Compulsions/Rituals

Addressing the way that you attempt to reduce your anxiety through the application of compulsions is as important as noting the obsessions that trigger them. When participating in exposure and response prevention, it is important that you not partake in rituals that you once applied in order to escape from your anxiety. Some therapists call this the 'banning' of rituals. Committing yourself to not participating in your rituals shows that you realize that they were only causing you more anxiety rather than abolishing them. Try to remind yourself of this when you feel the urge to participate in them if you are doing exposure therapy on your own.

3.12 In Panic Disorder

This form of exposure therapy intentionally cause anxiety and the physical sensations that come with it. People with panic disorder often associate the experience of certain physical sensations of that of an oncoming panic attack. Their fear of these sensations, in turn, will more than likely cause them to have a panic attack.

Like exposure and response prevention, interceptive exposure is meant to show the individual that the experience of anxiety in a physical manner is just that; the experience of something uncomfortable, rather than that of something that indicates doom.

Therefore, exposure exercise for the person with panic disorder will include many physical activities that stimulate a similar physical response that a supposed oncoming panic attack does. If you suffer from panic disorder, try participating in these exercises. Once again, try to rate the level of anxiety you feel next to the suggestion. Once you participate in one, observe yourself, and realize that the sensations are the result of actual physical exertion. They are always sensations that you can learn to cope with, not indicators of a bigger problem:

- Run on the spot for 30 seconds to 1 minute (will cause a racing heart, chest discomfort).
- Run up and downstairs for 30 seconds to 1 minute (will cause racing heart, chest discomfort).
- Shake your head from side to side, or move the head around by drawing a circle around you with your nose for 30 seconds (dizziness will be triggered).
- Spinning around in place for 30 seconds (dizziness and nausea may be caused).
- Stare at your hand for 2 to 3 minutes (feelings of unease, things looking 'weird' sensation).
- Wear a tight turtleneck or scarf around your neck for a few minutes (will create choking sensations).
- Tense as many muscles in your body as you can for 1 minute (can create muscle stiffness and soreness).

If you are planning on undertaking these exposures, include someone in their planning, like a close friend or parent. Try to engage in at least one day. Once you have physically induced similar anxiety-like physical sensations, observe your automatic thoughts that long to control your sensations. Often the fear of a heart attack or death will arise in you if you have been suffering from panic disorder for a long time. Instead of following those thoughts and trying to control the sensation, choose to notice the sensation, and do nothing to control it. Write down next to the activity how you felt when you chose not to control the sensation.

Once you begin to make it a habit of exposing yourself to these sensations, you will begin to create a new association between the normal experience of them and your mind; one that is indifferent and more realistic.

3.13 In Social Phobia

The experience of social anxiety disorder or social phobia is greatly associated with the experience of the physical symptoms that accompany anxiety. A person with social anxiety not only fears the particular situation but also the possibility that the expression of their anxiety might be seen by others and cause them to be embarrassed. Many people fear that they may be seen shaking, sweating, stuttering, fiddling, or breathing heavily. So there are two sides to this form of anxiety that go hand-in-hand. Interceptive exposure aims to once again, help you learn that you can experience anxiety symptoms and that you can indeed cope with them in a social situation. Some suggestions for this form of exposure would be to induce sweating before a social engagement, or going to the store after having too much caffeine to induce shaking. This shows you that even if anxiety symptoms are present, it does not necessarily mean that people are going to notice them. It also means that you are more than capable of coping with the symptoms.

3.14 In PTSD

Post-traumatic stress disorder is an anxiety disorder that associates the sensation of physical symptoms with a previously experienced trauma. Similar suggestions to those that were made for the person with panic disorder will be made for those with PTSD. People with this disorder fear the experience of their physical symptoms as it relates to their particular trauma. They are often overly sensitive to anything that causes physical arousal, such as loud sounds, or even people yelling. The exposure will be very specific to the person's experienced trauma and will be drawn out in a systematic manner, in a safe place with a person the individual feels safe with around. Other forms of therapy, along with CBT, are important in the treatment of PTSD and should be undergone with the presence of a therapist.

3.15 In Generalized Anxiety

People with generalized anxiety disorder have general worries about life, death, finances, relationships, children, travel, etc. The form of interoceptive exposure therapy that would be applied depends upon some of the main themes of anxiety you may possess. A therapist may ask you to drink coffee to induce racing thoughts, to show you that you can cope with the physical sensations of anxiety.

The entire point of this form of exposure therapy is to separate the cognitive association many people with anxiety disorders have with the experience of physical sensations. The experience of physical sensations is secondary forms of anxiety that piles upon the already large pile of triggers most people with anxiety disorders may have. But it is very important for you to engage in this form of therapy with another person around, along with the approval of your medical doctor. Some people may have other physical conditions that would render this form of therapy less useful.

If you do choose to engage in this form of therapy, use this worksheet as a reference so you can note down how you feel in response to each event of exposure (from PsychologyTools)

3.16 Anxiety: Interoceptive Exposure

Interceptive exposure is yet another form of exposure therapy that is mostly meant for those who suffer from anxiety disorders, panic disorder, and post-traumatic stress. It focuses mainly on how one can cope with the physical sensations that come with the experience of a panic attack. It has also been used as a method to stimulate anxiety in those with social phobia, generalized anxiety disorder, or those who have panic disorder with an accompanying medical condition.

3.17 Imagined Exposure

Imagined Exposure is a similar form of exposure therapy, but is taking place in the person's mind as an exercise rather than in the situation (commonly referred to as 'in vivo' exposure). There are many forms of imagined exposure exercises that can help many people who suffer from anxiety, depression, and anger issues.

3.18 With Anger

Both anger and anxiety are associated with accompanying physical sensations. Like the experience PTSD, exposing oneself to an anger-inducing situation is not always feasible once treatment first begins, especially when a person has immense difficulty controlling their reactions. People with issues with anger would benefit from recording interactions that are either from the past or interactions that they anticipate. Imagined exposure to anger issues would be helpful to appear like story writing.

If you suffer from anger issues and would like to engage in imagined exposure, refer to your list where you wrote and rated the top five situations or anticipated situations that you feel will trigger yourself most intense anger. Begin with the lowest anger-inducing situation. Start writing a description of what you may have already done, or how you anticipate the situation occurring. Write it down without anticipating your own reactions. Now, try to imagine the situation just as you described it. Think of a person, place, or thing, as vividly as you can. Allow those feelings of anger to rise inside of your body. Once you have gone through the entire interaction, try to take a step back and allow yourself to calm down. Once you have calmed down, try to think of a more rational, reasonable reaction to the trigger. This can act as great practice in the case that the situation occurs once more, or if it is something you are anticipating. It will also give you the confidence to feel like you are in control of the situation, rather than feeling hopelessly controlled by your anger issues.

3.19 With Anxiety

The process undergone to participate in this form of exposure is very similar to that of in vivo exposure:

1. Create a hierarchy of fears.
2. Rate them in order of most feared.
3. Begin with the least anxiety-inducing fear.
4. Expose oneself to the anxiety-inducing fear.
5. Monitor the experience of anxiety.

In imagined exposure, it is important to construct the scene of fear as vividly as possible. For this example, we will use a person who suffers from social phobia. Perhaps a fear that is lower on their hierarchy is going to the gym. Their fear has been divided up into 4 or 5 steps that they feel is required to get them inside the gym and to eventually exercise in public. The first step is to simply step inside the gym doors. Imagined exposure is best conducted with another person, or therapist, who can detail the experience while the client sits with their eyes closed and projects the experience in their mind. The therapist describes the experience as vividly as possible; sounds, smells, touches, possible interactions. The client is asked how they are feeling through the imagined scene. Sometimes the imagined exposure is recorded so the client can take it home and listen to the imagined exposure over and over again. Numbers are used to recording experiences of anxiety and progress down the line like that of exposure that will occur in person.

Imagined exposure is commonly used in conjunction with other forms of therapies for those with PTSD. In vivo exposure is often most feasible for people who have experienced trauma such as car accidents, physical or sexual abuse, or the observation of a violent event. Imagined exposure allows the individual to bring themselves back into the fear of trauma and to reconstruct their beliefs surrounding the incident.

3.20 Social Anxiety Disorder

In vivo exposure will involve many of the same steps that exposure and response prevention for OCD did. First, make a list of situations that make you the most anxious.

Start with the least anxiety-provoking, and rate the level of anxiety you may feel on a scale of 0-100. Your list might look something like this:

1. Walking past a big group of people: 40-50
2. Saying hello to my coworkers: 50-60
3. Using my debit card at the store: 70-90
4. Using public transit: 90-100
5. Speaking in front of a group: 100

Begin with the lowest level of anxiety that you believe you may feel while in that situation. In this case, it would be number 1, walking past a big group of people.

If the concept of doing this is too anxiety-provoking, try to break down the exposure into steps. In this example, it may involve slowly starting to walk by larger groups of people, or increasing the proximity in which you are walking near others. Your exposure breakdown may look something like this:

- Walk past two people at X distance.
- Walk past two people at a closer distance.
- Walk past three people at X distance.
- Walk past three people at a closer distance.

You could increase the number of people, to the point where it grows into an undefined amount of people, at which point it will not matter because you have learned that you are able to cope with your anxiety.

Your anxiety will only lower once you consistently participate in an exposure. The point of exposure is to feel the anxiety, and allow it to lower, which in psychology is called habituation. You will become adjusted to the experience because you have decided to no longer flee the situation.

For each exposure, write down the level of anxiety felt, and wait for the SUDS level to lower to a 30. Once the anxiety has gone down to a zero, you can move onto your next anxiety-provoking situation.

3.21 Generalized Anxiety Disorder

Once again, you will be asked to make a hierarchal list of your most anxiety-producing stations or triggers. For a person with generalized anxiety, the trigger could literally be anything. If you are able to identify themes within your anxiety, write them down, and then write associated anxieties that circle around them. For example:

1. Death: Death is a common theme amongst those with generalized anxiety. This person may also have panic disorder, which furthers the anxious theme that focuses on their own possible death. The person may also fear the death of their family members, loved ones, or even strangers. Unlike OCD, the person does not participate in rituals; instead, simply ruminates over the possibility of something horrible occurring.

2. Financial Loss: Many people worry about their career, how much money they have, how much money they will have, whether or not they will be able to provide for their children, etc. This leads to obsessive worrying without any proactive solutions.

3. Relationship Loss: A person may constantly worry that they are not enough for their partner in a relationship. They worry about them leaving them, finding someone else, finding things they don't like about them, etc.

If you are able to come up with these themes, or any other kind, write them down, along with the thoughts that accompany them.

In vivo exposure for generalized anxiety disorder is dependent about whether or not the exposure is feasible. For example, if you have a fear of death, a therapist may suggest that you go for walks in a cemetery, or to participate in activities that directly trigger the thoughts about death. Make a list of the things that make you most anxious, rate them between 0-100. It will depend upon your specific theme of anxiety as to what you will expose yourself to. But no matter what it is, it is very important that you begin small, work your way up, and not stop until the anxiety has lowered to 0 to each step.

3.22 In Vivo Exposure

'In vivo' is an expression used in CBT therapy that refers to 'in the moment' exposure. It is the direct opposite of imagined exposure. Imagined exposure is often used before in vivo, especially if an individual is very fearful or resistant to committing to exposure. In vivo exposure is direct conformation with the feared object or experience.

3.23 Simple Phobias

Simple phobias referred to specific fears of situations, objects, or animals; some examples would be the fear of spiders, fear of flying, fear of public speaking, etc. Simple phobias respond best to exposure therapy because they are showing the person that the feared outcome is not likely to happen, and that they are able to cope with the physical and psychological sensations that come with feeling anxious.

3.24 Other Forms of Exposure Therapy

The forms of exposure therapy that have been described in this chapter mainly pertain to those who suffer from anxiety disorders, and some for those that suffer from anger issues. Exposure therapy has not often been used for those who suffer from depression, but some research has been done to estimate that those with serious levels of depression could benefit from similarly styled exposure therapies.

Memory flooding and flashbacks are both key symptoms that those with PTSD and depression suffer from. A newer form of exposure therapy asks those with depression to look at the events that they feel may have helped trigger the beliefs that dominate most of their thoughts about themselves, such as uselessness and feeling worthless. A therapist would then ask them to reframe these triggers, asking them to look at them from a more positive light.

Although this is a new approach to treat those with depression through application of exposure, if you feel so inclined, try to look back on occurrences in your life when you have felt may have triggered these false beliefs about yourself, then try to reframe them from the perspective of someone who has nothing but positive things to say about you.

Exposure therapy is a daunting task, but for many people, it is a necessary fear to face in order to get your life back. It is important that you stay consistent with your exposures. It is going to be hard initially, but it will slowly get better, as you learn that you are more in control that your anxiety wants you to believe.

This chapter focused heavily on many techniques you can apply if you are experiencing a particular kind of stress-related disorder, or even you don't think you are quite there yet. The next chapter will look at the maladaptive outlets, some people who experience high levels of stress turn to, that in turn, only makes their life more complicated and thus, stressful.

Chapter 4: Addiction and Stress

All of us can relate to moments when we have had a particularly hectic workday, or a day that was emotionally draining, where we want to turn to a certain outlet that we know isn't exactly good for us. Grabbing a beer or two after work on a Friday after a busy week isn't really frowned up in Western society. Even getting very intoxicated from too much alcohol use on the weekends is accepted mostly. Using substances to help us relax is a common compulsion that many people can relate to one another with. It lowers our inhabitants, calms us down, and allows us to enjoy ourselves. People do this in other ways beyond alcohol, such as with food, video-games, sexual encounters, and other forms of entertainment. But there is a point when participating in a certain activity for reasons of stress goes beyond moderation, and thus, stops being healthy and average. When people fall into the pattern of overusing a substance or behavior in order to neutralize their feelings of stress rather than finding a healthy coping mechanism, they are at great risk for developing an addiction.

In a lot of ways, humans are very simple animals. If you eat, drink, or do something that makes us feel good, what could be wrong with doing it again? Especially when it provides relief from work stress, relationship stress, or even the stress of other mental health disorders. But what we don't realize we are doing is warming certain neural pathways in our brain that are associated with the reward system, and thus, conditioning ourselves to constantly reach for the drink/drug/activity that makes us feel better even at the slightest indication of discomfort (conditioning is the psychological phenomena that state how humans make negative and positive assertions with a certain actions, persons, places or objects—which often happens subconsciously and can be a difficult association to change).

Before we get into the concept of how stress makes you vulnerable to addiction and how to cope, let's talk about what addiction actually is.

4.1 What is Addiction?

As previously mentioned, addiction is a collection of behaviors and psychological associations between certain stressful feelings and thoughts that, when done consistently, turns maladaptive. When a person is in the depths of addiction, their entire lives are turned upside down, whether or not people externally can observe it. Their work lives, relationships, interests, and hobbies all become effected and corrupted by this activity that they feel is necessary to help them live their lives. What addiction essentially is being a maladaptive coping mechanism; it may start off as one or two drinks after work on the weekends, to them during the week, to five or six every day. People who binge drink may also be suffering from addiction issues because they are trying to block something out of their mind that is causing them great stress.

So instead of finding a healthy outlet such as writing, sports, acting, exercise, etc., to express their feelings of stress, this person has turned to something that is distracting and blocking out the stress, rather than looking directly at it. The reasons as to why certain people become addicted to a substance or behavior depend upon an abundance of personal factors, but what is common amongst all of them is that they haven't learned how to effectively handle stress. Stress in their lives could be caused by abuse, mental health problems, relationship problems, work problems, or a variety of issues that most people have experienced at least once throughout their lifetime. A combination of stressful life events and poor coping mechanisms makes a person more vulnerable toward developing an addiction problem.

What makes addiction so difficult to overcome is the fact that this person has created a habit about their assertion with any negative sensation. Through the use of their particular substance or behavior, the person has made themselves increasingly intolerant of any uncomfortable feeling. While it is normal to feel some level of stress and cope with it in a healthy manner, the person with addiction issues loses this ability to endure, diminishes their impulsive-control, and thus, seek out the euphoric relief as soon as possible. This behavior becomes patterned, and thus, done more often in order to keep gaining that positive feeling.

This book is not going to dive very deep into the various mechanisms of addiction or treatment options but will focus on a more generalized description and techniques that can be applied. If you or someone you love is suffering from an addiction issue, it would be best to seek professional help and advice for it.

4.2 Treating Stress and Addiction Together

Because stress has such a strong correlation with addiction issues, it would be best to focus on getting the treatment that helps you deal with both. Your addiction substance may have been your go-to for a very long time, so now you need to learn to replace it with healthy habits, along with various methods that help you realize that you can cope with the sensations that stress causes you.

1. Exercise: Exercise, in general, lowers levels of anxiety and depression due to the release of dopamine and serotonin, the positive pleasure neurochemicals. It also improves quality of sleep, diminishes cravings for your drug of choice, as well as lift your mood in general. All of this helps lower stress levels and makes it less likely that you will impulsively turn to your substance again.

2. Mindfulness and Meditation: Mindfulness will help you become more aware of the thoughts and

emotions that you associate with your addiction, as well as how you relate to the stress that makes you reach for your substance. Meditation can help teach you to remain calm with dealing with triggers for your addiction behaviors, as well as the feelings of cravings.

3. Behavioral Therapy: This will help you learn your own responses to certain situations and stimuli, and thus, learn how to change them. A specific kind of CBT called trauma-focused CBT helps people effectively cope with the stress associated with a particular trauma that may have caused an increase in stress in their life, and thus, substance use emerged.

4. Peer Support: It is very important for people with addiction issues to interact with people who have similar problems. It helps them avoid relapse and have someone of whom they feel close to that they can turn to, should they have any cravings or experience triggers.

5. Finding Hobbies: Finding a new hobby or going back to an old one will not only keep you busy but add the joy back into your life. If you have always wanted to paint, learning to sing, dance, or even

craft, recovering from your addiction may be the best time to start trying something new.

6. Healthy Routines: Getting up on the same day every day, going to bed at a healthy time, eat a well-balanced diet, and exercising are all examples of a healthy routine. These behaviors will act as the foundation for keeping up with your recovering because they will not only help you maintain structure but also help have less stress in your life.

If you don't feel like you are actively addicted to something that isn't healthy for you, take a moment to reflect on what you choose to turn to when you are feeling stressed. Do you vent to a loved one or a friend over a glass of wine? Do you decide to do a couple of laps in the pool after a rough day at work? Do you search for the nearest chocolate bar if you are feeling overwhelmed? In the area of your notebook where you wrote about your top stressful portions of your life, right next to them what you do to cope with them. This could even be an attempt to ignore them, distracting yourself by becoming overly busy with work, the kids, or some task around the house. All while any of these coping mechanisms aren't inherently unhealthy in nature, should they increase in volume and consistency, you could be at risk for developing an addiction. Try to pay attention to these behaviors and how often you participate in them. The key to this observation is not to judge you, but to help you become more aware of yourself. Noticing what you do to deal with stress helps you realize whether or not you are effectively coping with them, which involves facing the stressful event/person/thought at some point, or are actually only trying to distract yourself and run from them. Eventually, you are going to have to face whatever haunts you, because if you don't, it is only going to continue to press on you in more unique and subconscious ways.

Chapter 5: Negative Thinking Within Relationships

Perception is a reality, and each of our realities is shaped by our most practiced methods of thinking as well as our beliefs. When we think of negative or unhealthy ways, as we've seen, we cause ourselves unnecessary stress. But whatever happens, when these negative thinking patterns start affecting others, specifically, those that we are closest to in our lives? You may not know it, but the way that you think about yourself, the world around you, and others may be negatively affecting your relationships. Because of the ways that we were raised, ideas in the media that are driven into your heads, as well as unhealthy coping mechanisms, there are some subconscious notions about our partners or important people in our lives that may be forcing their quality downhill. Here are some examples of some subconscious thoughts/beliefs we may be harboring inside our stressed-out minds:

1. "I can change my partner by focusing in on what I don't like about them.": Many people have issues in their lives that causes them to want to 'fix' another person in their lives. This is often the case in

romantic relationships, where one partner may hone in on some aspect of their personality that they do not approve of. The more we focus on the negative aspect of a person, the more that that is all we will end up seeing. This, of course, is not fair or rational, and can greatly affect how the other person thinks you see them. Communicating a certain behavior that may both you effectively are healthy, but making a person feel ashamed about it is not.

2. "My partner knows I love them, so I don't have to tell them or show them regularly.": Once we start assuming in relationships and taking things for granted, a relationship may start heading downhill. If a person doesn't consistently see behavior that shows them how much their partner appreciates them, then they are going to start believing that they don't.

3. "My partner loves me, so it is ok for me to treat them badly sometimes.": We do tend to treat those that we love the most, the worst out of anyone else that we interact within our lives. This behavior is incredibly irrational and takes a lot of mindfulness to start noticing and correcting. When we know someone well, we worry less about what they may think and thus act out in more ways compared to if

we are just meeting someone. This behavior is selfish and doesn't take the other person's feelings into account.

4. "I'm right, and they're wrong.": This is a common issue in many relationships. We all perceive things differently, so there always isn't a 'right' way to understand something. A relationship is about two people, so only taking in the considerations of one isn't logical. You will learn much more by staying open-minded and listening to your partner's needs.

5. "Our relationship will take care of itself.": This is one of the biggest lies we tell ourselves within a relationship. Relationships take work as people, situations, and environments all change. If you stop making an effort, they will stop growing.

6. "They should know what I need and what I'm thinking—I shouldn't have to tell them.": This is also a very common subconscious thought that makes us angrier and disappointed at people we are in a relationship with than we need to be. Communication is a wonderful thing, and we need to learn how to use it more effectively to relay what we truly what from our partner.

7. "I expect everything to be fair.": Believing everything 'should' be fair in your relationship is

unrealistic. It isn't always going to be 50/50, because one partner may need more attention or support in their life vs. the other partner of whom may need it less at a certain point. Trying to constantly make the scale even will only frustrate both partners at some point.

8. "It's never my fault.": Constantly blaming your partner when something goes wrong in the relationship doesn't allow you to grow, or learn how to self-reflect. Being in a relationship, a healthy one, forces us to take responsibility for our actions. If we are always blaming our partner, they may begin to start thinking that this relationship isn't going to work out.

These are many faulty beliefs and negative thinking patterns that are capable of effecting a romantic relationship. Now we will list ways in which you can alter these ways of thinking, specifically in relation to your romantic relationships:

1. Managing Expectations: Some people think that disagreements and arguing mean that a relationship is not going to work out. But in reality, putting two different people together in close proximity is

eventually going to cause some form of conflict, because the two people are trying to figure out a way to support and thrive together and in their independent lives. Try to remember, if you have a tendency to worry and ruminate, that arguing is normal. What matters most is how you and your partner choose to resolve the issue, grow, and move forward.

2. Your Partner is a Person too! All human beings are flawed in some way. Think of yourself; if someone was constantly searching for things that weren't perfect in you, you would feel pretty bad about yourself, right? So try to remember this for your partner too. If something they say or do disappoints you, try not to let it be the be-all-end-all of your positivity towards them. Communicate your needs and try not to generalize a single experience of behavior as their entire personality.

3. View Them in a Positive Light: Be grateful for the little things that your partner does, acts of kindness and love. This makes you want to reciprocate, which makes it a cycle of optimism and compassion within your relationship.

4. Don't Take It Personally: For more sensitive people, or people with lower self-esteem, it may be harder

not to taking something your partner says or does in a way that seems intended to hurt. There are going to be bad days, hard conversations, and moments that feel painful. But instead of categorizing them as negative, try to look at them as an opportunity for growth, and to learn something new about you and your partner.

This advice doesn't mean that you ignore behaviors or actions that are hurtful. All these suggestions as of you are to become more mindful of your behavior, emotions, and thoughts, and how they could be adversely influencing your impression of your relationship. You still need to communicate and assess the results of the communication with your partner. No feelings are invalid.

Chapter 6: Habits that Relieve Stress: Behavioral Techniques

This is the section that will focus on the behavioral aspects of relieving and managing stress in your life. Since you have become mindful of the various ways that your thinking habits may enhance your stress, you can now learn how to integrate these new thinking habits into behavior that is healthy and less stressful.

We are going to focus on several suggestions, backed by psychological research, that help a person deal with stress, as well as how to relieve it. We are also going to dive deeper into techniques that help you become a more organized person, ways to learn how to schedule yourself, and how to apply various tactics of assertiveness. Learning how to do these things for yourself will lower the unnecessary amount of stress that you have in your life, so you can create space for self-care and relaxation, as well as time to develop ways to cope with unexpected stress.

6.1 Ways to Relieve Stress

1. Through Exercise: Exercise is one of the important things a person who is easily stressed can do to help them feel relief. The benefits are strongest when you do it consistently, s it may be helpful to start walking or running for at least half an hour, for 3 or 4 days a week. You will notice your mood changing and stress lifting pretty quickly! The physiological reasons behind the diminishing of stress due to physical activity is because you are lowering the amount of cortisol in your body, and releasing the pleasurable, painkiller like chemicals, dopamine, and serotonin. It also improves your quality of sleep, which can greatly affect the impact and intensity of stress and anxiety. You may also start feeling more confident about your body, which adds to the feelings of general well-being. Try something that doesn't feel like work initially, so you won't feel so put off so fast.

2. Try Supplements: There are many natural supplements that can help you cope with chronic stress. Here is a list of some of them that you might consider trying out:

a) Lemon Balm: This is a member of the mint family and has been used and studied for its anti-anxiety effects.

b) Omega-3 fatty acids: Students who received omega-3 supplements experienced a 20% reduction in anxiety symptoms during an exam in the United States.

c) Green tea: Provides antioxidants that provide general health benefits, and helps lower stress and anxiety for increasing serotonin levels.

d) Valerian: Valerian root is a popular sleep aid due to its tranquilizing effects. It contained valeric acid, which alters the receptors of the GABA receptors in your brain, to lower anxiety.

3. Reduce your Caffeine Intake: Caffeine is a stimulant that is found in coffee, black teas, chocolate, and energy drinks. It is easy for us to fall into the habit of drinking too much coffee, especially if we work in an office setting. Caffeine limits are different for everyone, but if you notice yourself feeling jittery, extra anxious, or are ruminating after several cups of coffee, try to start limiting yourself to 2-3 cups of joe a day, and take note of how you are feeling.

4. Write it Down: Writing down emotions, thoughts, and behaviors have been heavily emphasized throughout this book, and in good reason. Writing about what is bothering you will help you reflect upon what has been going on in your life. It will also help you get out that stress, using the act of writing as an outlet. Some people also find it beneficial to start writing about what they are grateful for when they are feeling stressed. This helps you focus on positive aspects of your life as opposed to the negative ones.

5. Spend time with Family and Friends: Being with those who love you no matter what is naturally going to ease your stress. When we interact with those we love, the love hormone oxytocin is released, which helps relax our bodies and minds. Make the time for those that help you feel good and forget about what might be bothering you in your life.

6.2 Becoming More Assertive

There is a big difference between being aggressive and controlling, then choosing to be confident when validating your needs and desires. Therefore, there is a difference between expressing anger aggressively and assertively. Expressing your anger assertively means that you are able to express how you feel while being in control of the feelings you are experiencing. Learning to express yourself assertively means separately how you feel with how you express yourself.

If you are having difficulty identifying the differences between being assertive and being aggressive, try to read over this basic summary:

1. Assertiveness is based on balance: It requires being straightforward about your wants and needs, while still considering these wants and needs of others. You are still applying empathy while firmly getting how you feel across to another person.
2. Aggressive behavior is based on winning: You focus solely on what is in your best interest without thinking about the needs and desires of others. The power you are applying while being aggressive is strictly selfish. You will come across as being a bully or pushy.

<u>MindTools</u> identifies seven suggested steps that you can follow if you want to develop your assertiveness skills. Applying these will help you to feel more balanced:

1. Value Yourself and Your Rights: Before you try to become more assertive, you should gain a better understanding of yourself. You should also try to develop a strong belief in your natural value of self, as well as your value within a team. Confidence is important when trying to be more assertive, but try not to allow it to turn into a sense of self-importance. Your needs, desires, and rights are just as important as everyone else's.

2. Voice Your Needs and Wants Confidently: If you want to perform at your best level and feel happy in life, you need to make sure your needs and wants are met. Try to identify the things that you want and need now. Set goals (as mentioned in the previous section) so you can look forward to achieving them. Once you have done this, it will be easier to express to those what it is exactly what you need or want. Remember to ask politely, stick to your point, and not to ask others to sacrifice their own needs for yours.

3. **Acknowledge That You Can't Control Other People's Behaviors:** This is an important fact for those with anger issues to realize. Oftentimes, we become angry with people when they do things that do not line up with what we want. But we cannot control what other people do, and it is important to keep reminding yourself of that fact. You can only focus on your own behavior. As long as you are respecting the needs of others, then you have the right to say what you want.

4. **Learn to Express Yourself in a Positive Way:** Falling into negative behaviors and expressions of anger is very easy. Try to focus on expressing what you need positively, even if you are feeling angry. This will help you not fall into the bad habit of name-calling, accusing, etc.

5. **Be Open to Criticism and Compliments:** Try to develop the skill of accepting both positive and negative feedback. Sometimes, when you receive negative feedback, it is easy to start feeling defensive and even hurt. If you do not agree with the feedback you are receiving, then you need to prepare yourself to say so. Again, this is meant to be expressed assertively, without anger or aggressiveness.

6. Learn to Say No: People who suffer from issues when being assertive often have difficulty saying no. Saying no is important when considering your own wants and needs, as well as contracting boundaries that are healthy and necessary. You are not able to please everyone, nor are you and endless source of energy. Saying no to people in your relationships, job settings, and friends show that you know what you want and need, and respect yourself enough to follow through on them.

7. Using Assertive Communication Techniques: There are a number of ways that you can apply certain assertive skills through the practice of some of these techniques:

    a) Use "I" Statements: Using the word "I" conveys the basic assertion that you want to get your point across firmly. It also avoids blaming and the escalation of pointless arguments.

    b) Empathy: It is hard when you are angry to try to see the issues from another person's point of view. But if you practice empathy on a consistent basis, the level in which your anger reaches will begin to lower each time you feel you are going to overreact. If you see a situation from another person's point of view, it is easier to understand the reasoning behind their behavior. You still don't have to agree with the person, but it will help your anger feel more constructive rather than destructive.

c) Escalation: Trying to be assertive with another person isn't always going to work the first time you apply it. Maybe that person also has issues with anger and expressing themselves/Some problems also require more time and patience in order to be resolved, such as problems in the workplace. If you feel you need to escalate your assertiveness, continue along the path of being polite and respectful, but firm.

d) Ask for more Time: If you can feel your anger rising and identify that you are having trouble controlling it, feel enough confidence to ask for some time so your anger can dissipate, and you can choose a reaction that is more rational.

e) Change Your Verbs: Try integrated verbs into your vocabulary that clearly and firmly state what it is your asking for, or what it is that you need. When you do this, there will be more room for misinterpretation. Begin using words like "will" instead of "could/should," and "want" instead of "need," "choose to" instead of "have to."

f) Don't be afraid to sound like a Broken Record: Keep reiterating yourself if a person is not taking what you are saying seriously. Continue you using the strong and firm message until the person will realize that you are drawing a line and are meaning what you're saying. This is best to practice at work if you are overwhelmed with tasks, and someone tries to throw more onto, using guilt as a weapon. No matter what they say, stick with your assertive statement that lets them know you cannot take on any more work. Your needs are important.

g) Try Scripting: Scripting is a technique that allows you to practice making assertive statements before you may need to state them. It will help you prepare what you are going to say, and give you enough confidence to stick to it:

i) The Event: Tell the other person exactly how you see the issue.

ii) Your Feelings: Describe how you feel about the situation and express them as clearly as possible.

iii) Your needs: Tell the person exactly what it is that you need from them, so they do not have to guess.

iv) The Consequences: Describe the positive effect that your request will have for the other person if you need are actually met.

Write down the observe steps in your notebook if this is an occurrence you want to practice being assertive about. Applying assertiveness instead of being angry will, in the long run, help you in your relationships, your work life, and will help you live a more enjoyable and fulfilling life.

6.3 Becoming More Organized

Here is a list of the various ways that you can become more organized, so you rid yourself of the extra stress that you are feeling in your life. The following tips are more general and may overlap with the previously mentioned ways of helping you create new habits that will help your stress level.

1. Write Things Down: The human brain is not made to recall all information. There is only so much we can store in there. Try writing down important dates, grocery lists, ideas you may have for a creative project, and you will find that you start to remember them naturally without having to consult the sheet of paper.

2. Making Schedules and Deadlines: This was already discussed in a previous chapter, but it is safe to emphasize now; if you want to be a productive person, you need to adopt the habit of scheduling yourself. This will, in turn, help you become more organized in your life. Creating deadlines for yourself will also help you feel more productive because you actually complimented something! This energy will carry you forward in a positive manner, onward into the next goal or task.

3. Don't Procrastinate: This is, of course, a lot easier said than done. Learning not to procrastinate is a habit in itself. Putting effort into getting things done at the time that you designated will only make you

feel more confident about the next task at hand. You will feel less stress, and moving onto another goal will feel more compelling, rather than burdensome.

4. Give Everything a Home: It is easy to misplace things if you do not have an area in which you consistently put something. If you make it a habit to put your car keys in a bowl on the kitchen counter every time you get home, then you are far less likely to lose them. Keeping your life organized means keeping your things in the places they belong to. People who are organized keep order by storing things in the spot they designated for them. If it is something you use often, keep it out and in front of you, not miscellaneous, but specified, such as pens and pencils in a cup.

5. DE clutter Regularly: If you are a messy person, this is a habit that you have formed. So it is going to be a bit harder to change that around. Begin by choosing one area of your house/apartment a week, and declutter it, finding a home for everything that is vital to you. Once you have finished organizing everything, try to keep up this weekly habit, so you do not fall back into the routine of clutter.

6. Keep Only What You Need: More stuff means more mess. People who are organized only keep what

they need and really want. Having fewer things will help you to feel less stressed, as well as having fewer things to have to clean. If you have a lot of things and have trouble with this, try to write down the things right off the top of your head that you feel you need and want. Then write a list of the things that you own. Compare them, and begin crossing off the things that you know you do not need.

7. Stay Away from Bargains: Going for sales will make you more likely to buy things you do not need, just because they are on sale. Try to keep a list of the things you actually need, or really want. If you are going shopping, keep this list close by, but without money. Then once you return from your trip, check on that list and see if anything you say was on it. This will avoid the trap of impulse purchasing.

8. Delegate Responsibilities: Being organized means you have less to do, and most of all, fewer things that you more stressed. If you are filled with responsibilities and things to do on your to-do list, try to re-prioritize, or give the task for someone else to do. Watch the stress fall away from you as your list of things that are your responsibility becomes smaller.

9. Work Hard: If you want to stay organized, you are going to need to put in a lot of effort. As previously mentioned, changing your habits can take from three months to a year to completely change. Sticking with it is going to be difficult, so be ready to put your best organizational foot forward.

6.3.1 Learning to Journal

The importance of journaling is paramount when undergoing this journey. It acts as a way to note down the thoughts, when you have them, what external or internal event might be triggering them, the intensity of the thought, the intensity of the mood, how long it took to go down or fade away, and learning how to gauge the intensity of the experience through number scales. A series of templates and exercises will help you begin observing yourself for the first week of this 4 week understanding of yourself and symptoms. Feel free to photocopy the suggestions, or to scribble them down in your own format in your journal.

6.3.2 Types of Journaling

There are several types of journaling that could help a person who is suffering from mental health issues. People use journals to keep track of other portions of their life too, such as exercise schedule, medication schedule, and diet. This section will focus mainly on the several types of journaling that aid those with anxiety, depression disorders, or anger issues. This is what you will dedicate yourself too within the first week of your journey. Look at this step as the information gathering step, where fault beliefs, thoughts, feelings and behaviors are identified. This chapter will also include several other mood, thought, and belief templates that you can used to start noticing the link between your thoughts, behaviors, and beliefs.

6.3.2.1 Mood Journaling and Tracking Depression

A general mood chart can begin tracking your daily fluctuations of depression. This simple template allows you to look at the difference between your mood during the day and at night, what you did that day, and accompanying feelings of anxiety or anger, or the possible use of substances such as drugs and alcohol. The amount of sleep you can as well as the quality of it is important to note throughout the week of your observation.

The journaling portion of mood tracking can help you begin noticing some common themes, thoughts, and beliefs. Set yourself a certain time and place to do this, as well as a specific time limit. A good amount of time is about ten minutes a day. It is important to place a limit on the amount of time you are writing for, because anything unlimited may cause you to begin ruminating on the issues that are bothering you most in your life.

Ruminating is not an uncommon mental act for anyone with mental health issues. It is defined as the act of continuously going over a problem, thought, or occurrence without a proactive resolution in sight. You can write about anything; something that happened in your day, how you felt about it, what you need to do, plans you are making, etc. Once you begin doing this every day for a week you will begin to notice patterns emerging, as well as the fluctuation changes in your mood throughout a day.

6.3.2.2 The Bullet Journal Mood Tracker

This is another easy and simple tool to apply if you want to write out your own mood tracking journal in your notebook. This approach applies clarify, organization, and effectiveness. Creating your own tracker also shows you that you do possess your own sense of autonomy, and you are capable of monitoring yourself in order to better your mental health.

This suggestion is part planner, part journaling style. It can show you more concisely the connection between the activities you partake in and the associated mood that comes along with it. This system was created by Ryder Caroll, who needs to create a rapid logging process that takes less time to write than normal handwritten entries. These six components are some of the ore vital concepts of this journaling style:

1. Topics and Pages: A short and simple title that makes the section easy to identify.
2. Bullets: Helps organize those actions and entries into an event, a note, or task.
3. Tasks: This is marked in the chart by dots or symbols that signify whether or not the task has been completed, or moved.

4. Events: Signified by an O shape, shows date-related occurrences, that range from a positive social event to a negative interaction. The point is to keep the description as objective as possible, without personal, and emotional subjectivities.

5. Notes: Show with a dash; more details can be provided about the certain topics being written about. This can include facts, observations, and thoughts.

6. Signifiers: More symbols that can represent certain emotions, and thoughts regarding certain entries. For example, an exclamation point '!', may signify the urgency of an event.

The point of this kind of mood tracker is also to stimulate your creativity. Examples of bullet journal mood trackers can range from something as simple as a colorful chart, to something more artistically inclined that blends color with images of cupcakes, or gumballs.

Some visual examples to help you visualize are here: PositivePsychology.

It is okay if you are not feeling at your most inspired or creative or inspired; the simplest way to track your depressive mood and associated feelings to use the first chart suggested, or to create one in your own notebook.

Carve out a page or two for each day, and divide each day into several sections as follows:

1. Mood in the AM (1-5): Write about how you feel when you first wake up in the morning and begin your usual routine. You may be getting ready for work, taking care of the kids, or simply trying to find a way to get yourself out of bed. Rate your mood between the numbers 1 and 5; 1 acting as immensely down and depressed, and 5 acting as positive and joyous. Try to write a single word next to the number that highlights your overall feeling in the morning.
2. Mood in the PM (1-5): Apply the same rules to this section as mentioned above, but in the afternoon and evening.
3. Actions in the AM: Use this section to all about what you did in the morning. Again, it could range from anything to going to a grocery store, calling a friend, or walking your dog. Talk about the actions objectively, but pay attention to anything that may

have altered your mood, whether it be positive or negative. Make note of it here.

4. Actions in the PM: Same as above, for the afternoon and evening part of your day.

5. Thoughts in the AM: Make notes of thoughts that you feel were reoccurring throughout your morning. If it's easier, make small notes about your thoughts in a different area of your journal so you can remember them for later. Take note of thoughts that are demeaning, unkind, suicidal, or begin with the words 'should', 'could.' If you are ruminating about a past event, or feel anticipation for the future, make note of that as well. The point is to begin noticing thoughts that are thematic and reveal some cognitive distortions and faulty beliefs.

6. Thoughts in the PM: Same as listed above. Try to pay attention to your thoughts as you are falling asleep, so you can note of them in the morning when you wake up.

After you have written about reach day, as yourself a few questions that can greatly relate to your mood:

- Have I taken all prescribed medications today?

- Did I exercise today?

- How much sleep did I get last night?

Try to answer all of these questions as honestly as possible throughout your week. This can also help you track patterns in your mood and associated behavior.

6.3.2.3 Anxiety Tracking and Journaling

This section is more specific to those who suffer from primarily chronic anxiety. If you feel you fall into both categories, feel free to use both journaling templates suggested. It is important though to focus on the most pressing issue first, such as depression, before tackling secondary symptoms. Focus on one issue at a time, so you do not feel overwhelmed, and feel the desire to give up completely.

Anxiety journaling is particularly helpful because it helps you to begin noticing your triggers, especially if you are unsure about what kind of anxiety you have. For example, if you have agoraphobia and are not aware of it, your triggers would be being in public, with the fear of having a panic attack weighing heavy on your mind. Noticing the physiological and associated psychological symptoms of a panic attack can help a person identify the oncoming symptoms of a panic attack before it becomes full-blown and overwhelming. First, we will focus on the experience of panic attacks.

6.3.2.4 Keeping a Panic Attack Diary

This can be written down in your hardcopy journal, or spoken out loud on a voice recorder. You are attempting begin noticing what triggers your anxiety, and so you can more easily share how you are feeling with others, such as friends, family, and physicians. Here are some important elements of the panic attack that you can write down:

1. Physical feelings: As previously stated, people who are having panic attacks often feel as if they are having a heart attack. Excessive sweating, chest pains, tingling sensations, shaking, and shortness of breath are very common symptoms that are easily confused with a real medical emergency. Ask yourself after your panic attack what you felt physically during that experience. Once you write them down you begin noticing how many physical symptoms you actually have, and how common they are amongst those who experience panic attacks consistently.

2. Emotions and Thoughts: One of the most common fears experienced by a person who is having a panic attacks is the belief that they are dying, or not they are going to lose control/their mind. Psychological symptoms such as depersonalization and derealization are experienced when a person feels detached from their physical selves. This experience further validates the person's belief that they are actually 'losing their minds'. Write down the thoughts and emotions that you are experiencing while going through a panic attack. Did you feel disconnected? Were there other emotions besides fear within the attack, such as anger and confusion? Try to remember these feelings and thoughts and write them down in your diary.

3. Environment and Life Events: The area and situation you are placed in when you experience your panic can provide you with a fair amount of information on the things that triggered it. Through writing it down daily, you may begin to notice you have panic attacks around a certain amount of people, in certain areas like bus stops or malls, with certain family members around, etc. It is also important to reflect about whether or not you have experienced a recent large life change. Examples of these are a big

move from one city to another, being away from
your family for the first time, the ending of an
important relationship, a change at work, etc. The
areas and triggers of your panic attacks can help
you flush out what may be unconscious anxiety that
you have been repressing.

When you are writing about your panic attacks, try to
rate the experience of the panic attack on a scale of 1-
10. 1, being the most minimal experience of a panic
attack, and 10, act as the full-blown version. But this
number next to the description of the physical and
psychological symptoms you experienced while having a
panic attack.

There are several healthy coping techniques that you
can apply to help you deal with having a panic attack
that will be discussed later on in this book. For now, try
to observe the experience, as well as the current coping
techniques you apply in order to help yourself through a
panic attack, or even behaviors you apply in order to
avoid having one. Making similar notes down at the
bottom of each day that asks about the amount of sleep
you had the night before, whether or not you have

taken the proper amount of medication that day, or if you were able to get any exercise in that day.

6.3.2.5 General Anxiety Tracking Log

The experience of anxiety that does not involve the experience of panic attacks falls under this category. This chart involves similar sections like that of the depression log; the day and time, the situation, the accompanying thoughts, physical sensations, a 1-10 rating of anxiety, what you did about the anxiety, what you said to yourself, and finally how you would rate your level of anxiety at the end of the experience of it. This is a tracker that logs specific events of high anxiety rather than a daily summation of the period of anxiety.

An example created by the Cornell Health.

6.3.2.6 Thought Journaling

Taking note of one's thoughts is an important activity in the first week of this journey. Your thoughts, and the behavior that accompanies them, will make it easier to identify beliefs and values that may be embedded deep within your mind. There have been several templates and approaches suggested, but here are a couple of general thought tracking charts in case the others do not suit your interest.

The first show thought record is a plain example of how you can keep tracks of your thoughts if you are suffering from depression, anxiety, or anger issues. The final section alternate thought asks you to begin exploring the notion of other thoughts that may be more beneficial to your mental health than the one that triggered a particularly negative emotion.

If you cannot think of an alternate thought, try writing down what you generally do in response to the experience of this thought and accompanying emotion. It is important to notice maladaptive responses as much as it is important to being learning new, healthier responses in day to day living.

Beyond the act of recording thoughts, emotions, and behavior, journaling for a straight 10 minutes each day to write about whatever strikes you is healthy practice to begin cultivating. Sometimes, people with mental health issues feel like their brains are full and overwhelmed; try to use the journal and journaling techniques to begin pouring out that heavy sensation.

Although journaling is not a cure-all, it is a part of many components of mental health recovery that will help you overcome your suffering and maintain a content life. You slowly become more aware of what you are feeling, the thoughts you are having, and the external triggers that be present during the experience of these thoughts and feelings.

If you have finished your first week of thought, emotion and behavioral tracking, congratulations! You are on your way toward living a more fulfilling and joyous life. It is important to keep up this practice of journal in the process of your self-treatment, so you can be aware of triggers and setbacks. As you read onto the next chapters, and begin applying the tactics suggested within them, continue keeping a journal and dedicate yourself to writing for at least 10 minutes a day, as previously suggested. Before you begin the next chapter, read over your records, your journal entries, and try to highlight or circle some common themes. Try to notice ones that you feel are maladaptive and pushing you more toward negative thinking and behaviors. Be mindful of these as you read on, and feel free to refer back to them, should you become confused or stuck.

Taking notes, writing journals, and tracking yourself, is not about judgment; try to avoid self-judgments and to write objectively about your experience of your mental health issues within the private pages of your journal or notebook. The only person you have be sharing these entries will may be a therapist, a physician, or loved one of whom you trust. These individuals will not judge you, and are more than likely to commend you for taking a proactive approach toward your recovery. Journaling does not need to be a purely mental health practice, as it is often used by people who have already recovered from mental health issues and want to apply it as a positive tool within their mental health practice of maintenance. Try to keep this in mind as you write about your thoughts and experiences each day.

Chapter 7: Self-Care and Relaxation

This is the part of the book where you learn how to wind down. Calming down after an event that is over stimulating is just as important as learning to calm down after a stressful event. Integrating self-care behaviors as well as methods of relaxation into your daily life will help these experiences of stress feel less overwhelming, and heighten your ability to feel like you can cope.

7.1 The Importance of Self-Care

The notion of self-care is a trendy topic in the Western world these days. When some people hear the term, they think of relaxing in a hot tub with lavender candles surrounding them, or a simple day at the spa where you get completely pampered. While these are wonderful ways to relax, they are not the only ways, and not always financially viable. Plus, not everyone enjoys massages, or even having a hot bath for that matter!

Others may see the fad as indulgent, selfish, and simply just that; a fad. But mental health professionals have been talking about the importance of prioritizing yourself for years. Many people have grown up in societies and home environments that made them believe that sacrificing themselves and their own needs as a personal virtue that needed to be sought after. This is why the concept of self-care may be so hard for them to grasp because instead of thinking of other people, such as partners, children, students, strangers, clients, they are choosing to think of themselves and their needs. It may be difficult to get past the idea that they are 'being selfish.'

But self-care is immensely important and can be the difference between success and total burnout. It is essential for learning how to manage stress because you are taking the time to do things the effectively relieve or prevent stress from arriving in the first place. One of the main reasons why you may feel overwhelmed with stress is because you don't take the time for yourself at all. But now, it is time for you to acknowledge YOU. Try to think this way, especially there are people in your life who rely on you: "if there is no me, there is no we." What this is stating is that if you do not take care of yourself, how can you possibly take care of others?

There are literally thousands of ways that you can begin to apply self-care today. Some do fall under the category of seemingly new age notions such as burning candles in a bathtub, doing yoga, diffusing essential oils and meditating, while others are as simple as sitting on the porch and people watching, drinking some tea in a coffee shop, painting, or watching your favorite TV show without interruption. Make a list of things that you enjoy doing and the things that relax you. Try to do one of these once every day. It doesn't have to take too long; all that matters is that it is being done for you, and no one else.

7.2 Mindfulness

The concept of mindfulness goes hand-in-hand with self-care and meditation. Mindfulness is the cultivation of awareness of self—your emotions, your thoughts, your behaviors, and the way that you think about your own thinking. It helps you learn how to stop ruminating and to bring yourself back into the present moment, so you can thoroughly enjoy that moment. If you haven't made an effort for your own self-care in a long time, it may be harder for you to allow yourself to do that without ruminating, or going somewhere else in your mind. Mindfulness practices help you learn to observe your thoughts without judgment or criticism and to teach you how to begin cultivating compassion toward yourself and your experiences.

7.3 Mindfulness Meditation

Mindfulness meditation is not just meant for monks. Many people misunderstand what the point of mindful meditation is. An image of someone hovering over the clouds on a mountaintop is a commonly associated misconception. Mindfulness meditation is not practice meant for an elect few. It is meant to be practice by anyone and everyone, no matter what age or point they are in their lives. No matter how busy, stressed, anxious, angry, or unhappy you may be, mindfulness meditation will act as another tool to integrate into your self-care toolbox. It has been successful in helping people in the past reduce stress, anxiety, depression, and anger issues.

Depending on what kind of mindfulness meditation you are participating in, the practice will help you by focusing your attention either on a single repetitive action, such as breathing or encourage you to observe a specific portion of your mind. Some practices ask you to observe your thoughts without judgment or criticism, so you can learn that thoughts are just as they are; not you at all. It can also be applied to several activities that involve movement, such as walking, eating, or exercising.

7.4 Breathing Exercises: Slow Diaphragmatic Breathing

This technique sends a direct signal to the brain to let it know that it is safe. This practice is usually recommended to be done alone, either before you start your day or after it. You can apply it while you are in a situation that makes you anxious or are coping with memory or triggered depressive thoughts. But remember, you are not doing this to rid yourself of the anxiety. If you are doing it at the moment, remember that it is meant to have the emotion felt, and to remind you that you are safe.

1. From a comfortable chair with your feet on the floor, or find a place to lie down.

2. Place your hands onto your belly and allow them to rest gently.

3. Start by observing your breath. Try not to judge the pace in which your belly is rising and falling.

4. Begin filling up your belly with an inhale slow, so it starts to feel like a little beach ball or globe. Imagine a balloon being filled up. Do not do this roughly or too fast. Focus on breathing into your stomach, and not allowing your shoulders to lift as you inhale.

5. Breathe out slowly to the count of five. Try to do this as slowly as possible.

6. After the exhale, hold for about 2-3 seconds before you inhale into your belly again.

7. Breathe in and out this way and observe how your breath has slowed down.

8. Practice this for around 10 minutes.

This practice will work better if you try to do this twice a day at the beginning of your treatment. Try to do it at the same point of the day, every day. This is usually a good start for those who suffer from anxiety or anger issues.

Here is a simple exercise of mindful meditation that you can begin practicing now:

1. Find a quiet, comfortable space where you know you will not be interrupted or distracted.

2. Sit on a chair that is straight-backed, or sit crossed-legged on the floor.

3. Choose a point of focus; most people like to focus on their breathing at first. It can be the sensation of air moving in and out of your nostrils, your belly rising and falling, or a candle flame or meaningful word you repeated through the practice.

4. Distracting thoughts do not mean you are 'doing it wrong'. Your mind is like a monkey and is meant to be playing around. If you find yourself becoming distracted, do not be angry. The point is to simply bring your attention back to the selected focus of attention, no matter how many times your mind tries to run off.

7.5 Visualization

This is a guided imagery practice and a variation on tradition mediation that involves the imagining of a scene that helps you to feel calm. Each person will have a different scene that makes them feel calm; it can be a beach, a childhood home, or even just your bed at home. You can do visualization either on your own or with a therapist. Aids such as soothing music help some people visualize better, along with sounds that co-inside with your particular location.

Here is an easy visualization exercise that can help you get started:

1. Close your eyes. Be sure to do this in a place where you are not distracted or unsafe.
2. Find music, sounds, or rhythmic tones that will help your experience feel more authentic. These can be found through YouTube, or through a simple google search.
3. Picture your peaceful place as vividly as you can; make note of the sounds, sights, smells, feels, and tastes.
4. Some people lose track of where they are during a visualization, have heavy limbs, or begin yawning. If this happens to you, don't worry, it is a very common reaction.

If you are unsure as to which practice may benefit you most, try utilizing one day for the next week. You will then begin to notice which ones you feel more comfortable practicing or receive the most benefits from.

Chapter 8: CBT Strategies for Overcoming Nightmares

This chapter will focus on two specific kinds of approaches applied in CBT for those with very specific kinds of mental health disorder. Nightmare Exposure is a behavioral technique for those who suffer from frequent nightmares, where Playing the Script to the End focuses on those with anxiety who obsess about feared outcomes.

You don't really have to be diagnosed with a disorder to benefit from these techniques. Some people have difficult dreams at certain points in their lives, while others suffer from specific anxiety during a stressful point in their lives.

8.1 Nightmare Exposure

Some people suffer from nightmares for different reasons. Some people may have experienced a traumatic event and are dealing with the symptoms of PTSD, while others may have dealt with abuse, have other underlying medical conditions, or possess excessive anxiety. Nightmare exposure is exactly what it sounds like; a technique in CBT that helps you face you fears of your nightmares. It intentionally elicits the nightmare in waking life, and connects them to the most prime emotion felt during the nightmare. The client writes about it in as much detail as they can recall. The therapist then will ask what emotion you would prefer to have, and this is where re-scripting comes into play.

8.2 Re-scripting

This is a technique that is often used for those who suffer from PTSD, and allows them to gain control over the perception of their upsetting images. What it mainly underlines is the notion that we cannot change the past, but we can change how we perceive it. A new emotion or outlook is created to associate someone with the various images or themes of the memory or nightmare, so the sufferer can begin to feel more in control of what they are experiencing.

8.3 The Application of Nightmare Exposure and Re-scripting

Exploreable describes several steps that are necessary when emerging yourself into nightmare exposure and re-scripting. The steps are very similar to that of imagined exposure, a technique previously described. Follow along these steps if you are suffering from nightmares:

1. Confront Your Nightmares: The next time you have an upsetting nightmare, try not to ignore it. Dreams, like movies are stories, can be interpreted differently, and you are in control of that interpretation.

2. Look into the Abyss: Make sure that there are no distractions around, and begin asking yourself these questions: What was the worst part of your nightmare? Do your best to describe it, and write it down? Although this may be difficult, try to remind yourself that the more detail you describe, the more able you will be to associate the different images with a more helpful and positive emotion.

3. Focus on Your Experience: Now you can focus on the physical and psychological experience of the nightmare. Write down your physical sensations you either felt while experiencing the nightmare, and how felt immediately after waking from it. Write about how the sensations you felt differ from reality. This will help you separate experiences felt within

dreams and those felt in reality, which will make the experience less traumatic over time.

4. Dream vs. Reality: Consider an element of your dream, in regard to sensations and experiences, that stand out as not being elements of reality. Try to say these differences out loud so the differentiating can become more dramatic and real to you.

5. What would be a better feeling: Now you must focus on the negative experiences you had during your nightmare? Once you have that in mind, and have written it down, think about what experiences, sensations and emotions you would have preferred to have had in the dream rather than the negative ones that you did. Try to be very specific.

6. Change the Story: Using the details listed above, as well as details from your nightmare, to change the story, so it corresponds to what you want, rather than what you felt in your nightmare that you could not control. Turn scary events into something, change the location, setting, characters, anything you want. Make sure you write it down in as much detail as possible.

7. Visualize the New Story: Try to imagine your new dream as vividly as possible. The more you are able

to visualize it, the more your mind will become used to the story, and be more likely to reproduce it once you go to sleep. This is not going to work instantly though, so do not be discouraged. This may take up to 4 or 5 days for your new dream to manifest.

8. Always Start Small: As stated in previously applications of exposure therapy, it is best to start with the least anxiety-provoking nightmare, if you are susceptible to having different kinds of nightmares. Build up gradually to the ones that give you the most trouble.

The point of this exercise, as it relates to both nightmares and PTSD, tries to help the sufferer feel more in control of their experiences, rather than having their experiences control them. Dreams, flashbacks, and memories are not reality; they are the perception of a different kind of reality. This techniques help reframe an experience or dream so it becomes less and less likely to cause more psychological harm to the individual who is suffering.

8.4 Playing the Script to the End

This is a CBT technique that explores the possibility of the worst anticipated outcome. Many people who suffer from all forms of anxiety disorders anticipate terrible outcomes to many different kinds of events. A person with social anxiety fears intense embarrassment, or being called stupid in a public forum. A person OCD fears that if they do not participate in their rituals, then a member of their family may get hurt. Someone with generalized anxiety may fear losing the job and not being able to provide for their family. A person with a fear of flying thinks that if they fly, then they are going to die.

All of these experiences of anxiety have one thing in common; they are rumination about an imagined outcome, with very little to no rational exploring the possibility. If likelihoods of event applying statistics, or the exposure therapy applied that attempts to show that the feared outcome is not going to occur, does not work, then this technique may be helpful for you. It can also be used in conjunction with other techniques of CBT.

Instead of avoiding the concept of the worst outcome, or learning that the likelihood of feared outcome is low, these techniques asks you to actually look into the entire narrative should the feared outcome happen. It is meant to make you look at this feared outcome in a practical manner, and to identify when you may be exaggerating your reactions. Imagination is very powerful when it comes to our worries, and normally, should the worst happen, we are more than capable of coping with it.

This form of exposure therapy will go through similar sections as the Nightmare Exposure and Re-scripting. Read over the following questions once you have made your list of most feared outcomes, rating them between 1-100, on a SUDS level between 0-100. Write them out in a narrative style format, citing as many specifics as you can muster:

1. What's the situation that I'm worried about?: Do your best to be as specific as possible. If you have social anxiety, perhaps you are worried that when you are giving the cashier change, you are going to have shaky hands, and then you will drop the

change. Write about this occurrence with as much emotional detail as possible.

2. If that situation were to happen, what would that lead to?: If you did have shaky hands, and you did drop your change, what do you think that would lead to? You make note of how embarrassed you may feel, how anxious you feel, how you are beginning to worry about what other people are thinking of you, how you may hesitate to pick up the change, etc.

3. If that situation were to happen, what would that lead to?: The reiteration of this question is important, because it will continue down the path of the description. From here on out, you will follow this question until you arrive upon what you are truly fearing. In this situation, it is more than likely that you are fearing the opinion of others, that they make think you are stupid. Once you arrive upon that conclusion, keep asking yourself the above proposed question. If people in line did indeed think you were stupid, what would happen? Well, you would probably feel immensely embarrassed. Embarrassment is an emotion that is felt temporarily. But if you combine this with exposure therapy, where you are intentionally feeling the

emotion of embarrassment, you will learn that not only will this sensation dissipate, but you can be present with it, and cope with it.

Try to write out the absolute worst outcome of all of your anxieties, starting from the bottom, while following this process. This process is meant to show you that you are capable of applying practical measures should the absolute worst actual happen. This will help you build confidence, while identifying more realistic expectations that are not driven by your anxious thoughts.

Conclusion: Chapter 9: Preparing for Sudden Stress and Prioritizing Yourself

The entire point of this book is to help you rid yourself of unnecessary stress so you can learn to enjoy life more. That doesn't mean that you are never going to experience stress again. As mentioned, stress is a normal, human emotion, that when experienced too often, turns into unhealthy coping mechanisms, thinking patterns, and physiological effects. There is stress in our lives that are familiar, and hopefully, through reading this, you can have learned the difference between problem-solving, ruminating, and unhealthy ways of coping with those feelings of discomfort. But there will always be times when we deal with a sudden source of stress—being let go from a job, an injury, a death in the family, an upheaval of location, etc.—and we must be prepared to deal with that. Not prepared in the obsessive, anxious sense, but prepared enough to feel confident in our own abilities to cope.

Here are some ways that you can deal with sudden stress so you can move forward into problem-solving mode and start acting outwardly as soon as you can:

1. Labeling: Try to label the thoughts that fall under the category of worrying, of ruminating, of overthinking, etc. Worry has never helped anyone in their life; there is a distinct difference between worrying and problem-solving. In the moment of a crisis or sudden news, try to label the thoughts you are having as useless, (the worrying thoughts) and the ones that are useful (the action thoughts).

2. Thinking with Your Shoulder: Try to shift your stress to a part of your body that isn't used for thinking, such as your shoulder, hands, feet, or toes. This is a lot like the breathing technique mentioned, as you are focusing in on a part of your body rather than allowing your monkey mind to run off with you.

3. The Alien Technique: Try to think of yourself as an alien who has arrived in your body to help make your life better. You think about the alien noticing your life, and that you don' really have anything to worry about. This narrows down your worries into what is essential rather than what is pointless.

4. Tense Up: In a moment of stress, try to tense every muscle in your body for five seconds. Then relax them. This forces you into fight-or-flight mode and was in control of instantly relaxing it.

5. Breathing: Inhale for 5 seconds as your belly fills with air, hold for 5 seconds, then breathe out heavily through our mouth for 7 seconds. You are sending positive endorphins out of your brain, and you will soon start feeling relaxed so you can deal with the problem.

One of, if not, the most important aspect of this book is the point that forces you to start considering yourself a priority. You are feeling stressed because you have not done this for yourself, and you have not allowed yourself to take the time to learn how to get rid of it and cope in a healthy manner. But that time is in the past, and now is the moment to move forward, and allow yourself to enjoy the wonders of living a life that is stress-limited.